DONATO MANCINI

LOITERSACK

Evelyn,

One m, paid the
rent, read some laughter -
long day,

Vancouver | New ~~Star Books~~ | 2014

NEW STAR BOOKS LTD.
107 – 3477 Commercial Street
Vancouver, BC V5N 4E8   CANADA
1517 – 1574 Gulf Road
Point Roberts, WA 98281   USA

www.NewStarBooks.com
info@NewStarBooks.com

The publisher acknowledges the financial support of the Canada Council for the Arts, the Government of Canada through the Canada Book Fund, the British Columbia Arts Council, and the Government of British Columbia through the Book Publishing Tax Credit.

Cataloguing information for this book is available from Library and Archives Canada, www.collectionscanada.gc.ca.

ISBN 978-1-55420-085-6
Cover design by Oliver McPartlin
Edited by Louis Cabri

Printed on 100% post-consumer recycled paper.
Printed and bound in Canada by Imprimerie Gauvin, Gatineau, QC
First printing, October 2014

CONTENTS

Only biography. Face as close (memory)
An incident in the park called.
Epoxy Police. Kid on the swing yells
Ronnie scribbles, Ronnie enters a world
embarrassed. The woman with glue left,
indifferent to, and, doesn't smoke, got away
so to speak. Not a loose transcription but languaged
events. The end pulled through and the distance
allows telling. This not the business of telling
but the ever expanding entering the world (middle).

–Deanna Ferguson, *The Relative Minor*

THE YOUNG HATE US

Can poetry be matter?

Language as a kind of *Stuff* from which to make a *Thing*.

Vigorous verbs. Robust adjectives. Solid nouns. Greasy adverbs.
Slithering participles. Feminizing semicolons. Fruitwood. Soapstone.
Ebony. Agony. Chuck-eye.

◢

So, white space of the page as mimetic, abstract or temporal.

Pages bury easily under text, if there's a lot of it. Prose as a means of
textual reification. Prose means. Reification.

◢

What one does, then, when one is drawing one's poetry, is engage
the whole problem of Art through a process of diagnostic attrition.
Especially of agnostic diagnoses. Not the production biography of i.e.
what if I were to write [*an/a*]? Address oneself to the problem not of
one's art, but of *one art*.

◢

Recursive questioning and/or *negative iteration*.

Imperfectly synonymous terms. The problem for poets now is that poets
can do anything. Anything poets want. Principle of Plenitude is Crisis of
Plenitude. No such thing as writer's block. Light; sound; data.

Recursive questioning and/or negative iteration: feedback loops consuming the feedback as they turn. Block out a sequence of refusals – negate, eliminate – determine what the work will *not* do, manoeuvre it towards its final form.

◓

Bad poetry vs Good poetry. In a time when most marks are for coiffe, in a time when armpit deodorant is obligatory, in a time when dinosaurs walk the earth, when accountants run universal edification factories, clean copy is mistaken for good writing, and a certain lack of tidiness looks stylish.

◓

Cast the iron rigours of Great Poetry as afternoon days at the Rocky Balboa Masterworks Gym; the totally pumped steroidal bottom-line economics of Great Art.

◓

Poets as sales managers. "Do it well enough and you get to work in the New York office. Do it perfectly 20 years later and there might be some vending machines for you to re-stock in East St Louis." (A. Peter)

Visual poets concrete poetry. "I think we should all produce work with the urgency of outsider artists, panting and jerking off to our kinky private obsessions. Sophistication is conformist, deadening. Let's get rid of it." (D. Bellamy)

◓

Crowd = numbers and statistics

Community = real human relations

Who Addresses the Crowd Speaks to No Community.

Poets are the statisticians of false human relations.

◗

Don't mind if I. "Capitalism begins when you open the dictionary." (S. McCaffery)

Meaning is commerce, they say. Meaning is always on sale. Meaning is our product, we mean. We are full of it. We are words. Meaning is our business, business is slow. Yes, poets trade in meaning and affect, as painters trade in objects.

Tradesy grammar: Painters' products referred-to using the countable *a*. Yes, that's a real Signac. Certainly, that looks like a Motherwell. "Yes!" (P. Webb)

Product of poets is an uncountable significance, an effusion, a puss, a creamcheese. A foie gras from the poet's metrically disciplined guts. The poet is, by a-numeric grammar, a paste-maker.

Production-line, intestinal poetics. *Pasta knowledge milk cheese garbage news research.*

◗

All the issues. Every question ever asked by any poet, good, bad, forgotten, stupid, fish, irrelevant, French, yellow, rotten. Gives blush to cold cheek. Every issue at issue. Meaning: tissue. O, you mean palimpsest: you.

◗

It might be even simpler.

Poetry might just be language, which is
vocabulary
plus
a set of rules to run it through
which equals
language
which equals
poetry
which makes them
indistinguishable
and makes

◢

An object rendered aesthetic is functionally no different than a work of
art, someone said. Some *one* got a text-message, *ping*! Some *him* looked
at his watch but it wasn't in *his* language.

Happy Birthday. I stuff thee full of such watches.

Language looked at with a certain misrecognition   →

                                                    poetry.

◢

Tradition as Delta.

Axis of Ambiguity
Axis of Authenticity

Black Hats
White Hats
Them
Us
Good Guys
Bad Guys
The Moderns
The Formalists
Mainstream
Slipstream
Official
Orificial
Oppositional
Insiders
Outsiders

➤

And then there's the bloody (i.e. material) *Problem of Nothing*, which is nothing like saying nothing is problematic. Making nothing is a material problem; it matters. (**Nihilist bass-line.**)

A manifest, material device as arbiter, or determinant, or a blatant address to material conditions of meaning-manufacture, grants some *thing* to a poetry of the *no* thing.

➤

Cultural afterlife as dollar store. It's not about novelty.

For two cents, the use of arbitrary material restrictions in poetry forcefully conditions new linguistic possibilities.

For three cents, production-side, material devices/determinants break habituated patterns of language-use.

For four cents, consumption-side, the formal restrictions can alter habituated patterns of cognition and emotion, re-patterning (inner) lives.

Buy One Get One Free: devices foreground the material conditioning of structures of feeling, the girders of the mega-bridge of embodied meaning poetry-lovers daily negotiate, the nonarbitrary social effects of meaning-production.

Arial aerial-shot: Capitalism restricts our life options, why shouldn't poetry, too?

◗

"Grammatically

                modified realism,

genetically modified

      freedom. Redefined
      as 'product', we
      boycott ourselves." (C. Smith)

(Changing the world
one subjectivity at a time.)

◗

Every word was once a poem
every word once sad apart to pin so
sad as every word to go
to not go get sad not you
once sad to word to scratch it poem
too once too too
sad to word-sad mod too
old to go do all to
words once sad as total was
nor once sad as every word
when was was not a word yet
every poem once sold mud once words
so every very word-sad word
once was so so sad not so-so.

◗

To the music-lover who says "I like both kinds of music: country *and* western", do you answer "It's just a matter of taste" because taste is malleable, dissoluble, not a hard constituent of a person's subjecthood? Taste is an indice of an ideological constitution – the 50 to 75% water of social existence. To understand ourselves as subjects, we need to work backwards through taste, dissolving it by-and-by like superstitious fats, like burnt speech.

Good Taste (GT) is good self-discipline. GT is a militant self-interpellation into an inherited condition. The model music-lover above has only heard the kinds of music s/he's heard: both kinds. Good poetry – poetry as a social intervention – not just "quality stuff", offends GT, by directive. Erect no counter-myth. Or say: wear taste as a badge and wind up in a uniform.

◗

Armies of The.
Dawn of the Dead.
Syllabus of the Dead.
Day of the Dead.
Moment of the Dead.
Scrapbook of the Dead.
Tax Credit of the Dead.
Debts of a Dead Dad.
Will of the Dead.
Children of the Dead.

In other words, resniffing an old critical sweatsock, does the social moment of the poem freeze-frame at initial writing first publication first rejection slip or travel a yellow post-it note brick road of increasing recognition towards the undead media castle of dissemination, sporific joy of diaspora, geoduckesque bliss, achieving at last dreamed-of immortality as a culturally indelible transcendent cliché?

◗

Take your positions.

North of Heartbreak.

North of Boston.

North of Intention.

North of South.

North of the Beaufort Sea.

North of the USA.

◗

A modest to high degree of alienation serves the poet (*to become specific*).

A modest to high degree of vagueness serves poetics (*to become alienated*).

◗

Therefore.

Even More Possibilities versus *Absorptive Plurality*.

poem as

        hand-grenade

        head-grenade prickly pear

        human document

        humument

        notation of mind's movements

        testament

        testimony

        bib dribble

        witness statement

        rearticulation

        dearticulation

        description

        trinket

        puzzle

score of voice

scratch of violence

yawp

inkmarks

pixels

chart of the changing weathers of temperament

poem in

advance

of the broken

arm.

◗

verse form.
nonce form.
phatic form.

Phatic form (*is something I just invented*)! This is what phatic form is. It's not nonce form, nor nerdification-of classic venerated now inconsequent except in détournement verse form. Phatic form describes the many open quote, "poems", close quote, that stand in for poems, just as prose may stand in for news among advertisements, may be ads for news not present; i.e. sign *News!* without bearing anything news. Same, phatic form poetry represents Poetry. Its main order of signification is *Look at Me I Am A Poem Keeping the Poetical Soulfires Burning.* Only duty of the phatic function poem is to signal POEM as often as possible without saying "poem" too often because that would meta-harsh the marsh mellow. Whole books, whole careers, whole schools.

phatic oeuvre?

◗

What? A. Safe. Way. To? Write!

In an age of accumulation by dispossession, of neoliberal terror, of ransack and pillage.

●

If truth is salmonella rye in a culture of accountants, business people, customs officials, micro managers, metre maids, economic fundamentalists it's because tables of cultural know-know demand content to fill the forms and the distributors await product. Cultural placement of things is predirected at its inspection before the product is shipped off to enter the culture, which means, of course, when crossing the frontier from production-side to consumption-side certain duties apply.

Duties: a poem must, a poem must also, a poem must then, a poem has to not only show what a war is like but show the conviction of death.

A poem must work for a living.
A poem must also be valid.
A poem must then speak for itself.
A poem has to be a poem.
A poem needs to move fast.
A poem needs to include contradictions.
A poem should be palpable and mute.
A poem must have the properties we know poems to possess.
A poem should be but not be mean.
A poem should palpitate.
A poem has to have enough money for a serial train ticket.
A poem has to go where it will.
A poem must sing out of itself and carry magic.

A poem must make its own world and by inference its own World Trade Organisation and therefore maintain low international labour standards in order to keep cultural economy in boom and/or avert market collapse.

The right truck carries the right goods along the right track. The eager Truth Officer carries the right instruments – necessitating itemisation, listing, fact-finding, check-listing of must-haves:

100% AUTHENTIC FOR NOW.

◠

If you know what the poem's job is you should ask who the poet's boss is.

◠

"I'm just a prole whose intentions are skewed
Oh Lord, please don't let me be understood." (E. Burdon)

◠

Exchange value = testable knowledge
Use value = untestable knowledge

◠

Who tells you poetry speaks for itself, that person speaks for poetry.

No good poetry without good readers, no good readers without good writing about reading.

◠

Writing was not implicit in language, writing was implicit in mark-making; the capacity of one substance to alter the surface of another.

The toddler who flings *SpaghettiOs* at the white wall performs a primary act of writing. Writing is pre-graphemic.

Did ancient teenage poetry-lovers get it together to build Stonehenge before they discovered that gull shit sticks to boulders, that berry juice stains fingers?

Writing is not language. Writing came first.

◗

Intellect as sausage machine – "literaturwurst" (D. Roth). Bildungs literaturwurst. Anectotal.

The problem of intelligence is what people have, how to use what people have. Intelligence, will, power. A fiercely a-demanding discraft of unverse makes poets will-powerful in intelligence-use.

Our defined problem being: intelligence, use of. Intelligence, application of. Appetite. Intelligence as trash-compactor. Solid cubes of impeccable correctness, stable in relation to the facts of the world, "the world" a square frame the cube fits through to plop back into The Real World.

The problem, also, of intelligence as lawnmower. Appearance of process + result = copious clippings unprocessed but well gone-over. Some minds are as three lawnmowers roaring at once on three different terraces.

◗

Just past what's masterable, just past what's knowable therefore exchangeable. Wire the poem to make your own brain explode. Confound mastery as you acquire it. Learn more than you can. Cram. Outwit yourself. Take the rational principles of a financialised daily life many air miles too far.

Burst the pipes of everyday reason.

Eat the anec-tote-bag itself. And the shame. Spread it like sham.

◠

incomprehensibility ≠ absurdity
ambiguity ≠ lack of commitment
& ≠ ≠ ≠

◠

"Duckwalking a Perimeter" (K. Davies)

"Art remains interesting
only so long as
a hope remains
all artists are
quacks." (C.Butterfield)

◠

"Belief in the value of the work of art [i.e. the poem] is part of the full reality of the work of art." (P. Bourdieu). No resistance, no essence further. Poetry is and can only be texts that are read as poetry. Weird splooges of ink viewed as traces of poetry's passage. Quality? None. Only value. This is what poetry functionally is: a system of value and valuation.

Belief in quality as essence of or as properties of, lingers in precisely the same way that vestigial superstition lingers in atheists. Phantom appendix; operation; cure.

◠

Genre isn't the issue, except the poetic risks becoming merely the operations of *genre-as-pattern* when readers' and writers' fulfilled expectations are too specific. When the poetic experience, the particular magic of poetry, the poetry buzz, yellow mist whatsoever, is too recognisable – if not articulable – poets start writing Poetry. Readers then come to expect a certain kind of bump from it and believe there's an *it* to bump. Poetry becomes: *Meet Me At The Genre*.

Poetry-lovers should not be pleased to recognise the poetic so easily. When they do, poetry becomes one of many fine luxury goods – organic red wine or unsweetened apricot jam. Poetry loses its criticality, loses its vital otherness. Loses social pertinence. Loses its power.

Phatic genre? Might as well take the copper wiring and the 60W lightbulbs, this place is going to be torn down anyway.

Mere discourse? Mere spectacle? Mere affect? No: bricks punch back the martial fist.

"You can crush us, you can bruise us, you can Guattari and Deleuze us but oh no: guns of Brixton." (P. Simonon)

Poetry now as a triangulation of

music

contemporary art   social critique.

Music not so much as sound, but as structure, architecture, temporality.

Contemporary art not so much as visuality, but as concept, practice, mood, value.

Social critique as the base of any vital poetics.

Poetry against metaphor. Metaphor is: let's make dividends in the bull market of our moist embraces. Visual poetry. Against metaphor. Against description.

Punctuation: mark as a syntax.

Reality in poem.

Reality of poem.

Reality | Poem.

Reality | poem.

Reality → poem → Reality.

Reality, poem.

Reality/poem.

Reality. Poem.

Reality poem.

◗

"It's beautiful, but where are you going to put it?" (J. Cage's mom.)

Department of English Department of Poetry Department of Drama
Department of Want Ads. Disciplinary slash disciplining categories as
contingent, impermanent, convenient, sociological fictions. Fictions
unrelated to the structuralist slash formalist character of mark-making.
Of writing. Transdisciplinary writing and visual writing jettison
institutional suitcases. Lead and feathers. Department of English
Department of Poetry Department of Drama Department of Want Ads.

What except habit could make [*it*] not poetry?

◗

Psychedelic. Cementitious.

Visual poetry, unhooked from the instrumentality of design or the
discursive histories of contemporary art. Most visual poets aren't making
images, they're making visually over-coded texts that push the student
loan debt Poetry Master back into alphabetic pre-school. Here.

A. B. C. D. E. F. G. H. I. J. K. L. M.
N. O. P. Q. R. S. T. U. V. X. Y. Z.

The needs of art and poetry now: no return to disciplinary boundary, or generic specificity, or media purity. Open poetry to basic questions that affect all communication, and (therefore) all art-making.

"What appears as eclectic from one point of view can be seen as rigorously logical from another [...] practice is not defined in relation to a given medium [...] but rather in relation to the logical operations on a set of cultural terms, for which any medium – photography, books, lines on walls, mirrors, or sculpture itself – might be used." (R. Krauss)

WHISPER SWEET NOTATIONS

Don't
throw out the baby with
the LSD accelerator.
Ash dust lips
of the memory-hole.

No joke
is too stupid.
I

want this job because
I have a passion for toxic waste.
Stay out of my
wiggle-room. I am
the last individual, best advantage.
Inexplicably

modernist, he wore
the type of shirt seen only
at jazz festivals. Remotely.

If art
can reside
in idea, the poetic
may inhabit
icon, sign
or mark. Context

of a greater social good
only. Who
was the first author? Sight
of struggle – slogan,
fence, traffic

cone. Find great work
in the cultural sphere
via *Labour Ready* – an

evil homology. 1 or 2 scoop
gelato? Escape into leisure
hours with good company

instruction manuals.

Joe Poetry

knows what he wants.
Do you know what you want?

What if Joe Poetry finds out
you don't write for him?

Signs of ubiquity.
The first contemporary
artist. Seer of Prague
our go-to guy. For?
In the name of contradiction

and diversity. And lust.
Foregrounded in the body
of a mass media. Poetry
displaced by
post-mortem

postmodern
amusements.
Nothing's good as
a Rorschach artist

cleaning his brushes.
Wishes fulfilled
alienation healed
petals fall
on Petaluma.

An epic
of public transit proportions.

*Illiterate
billionaire?*

Real sex-machine of an Italian
Marxist. or French.
Wrote in prison.
Wrote from prison. "Person" as

limit of the representable
as in: "Videostore clerks
are always so cute."
Secular documents galore
as in: "My mom's recipe

for disaster
written in blood
on the altar
of denial."
For a moment,

stung into introspection, I am.
Soft-focus slo-mo *Bildungsromane*
shelved high with "moral erotica."
Orgasms of righteousness
out of reach
not long;

more literate
than they think they are.
Audience, incertainties.
Entertainment

Tonight. I'd like to switch
to binge drinking.
Do you think
Marxists should sleep on the floor

in fear?
Can't see the gravestones
for the ghosts. Vantage
point. Voyage-point.
Vintage Pinot Gris.

Everything has become
money.

Except
language.

Start...
... ...
... now.
The game doth
not wait, Lexington.
Learn from

other people's mistakes.

Peoples.
These.
Countries.
These traditions.
These civilisations.
These villages.
Kind of scary
if you sit around and think about it.
Live off

THE FAT OF THE TEXT.
Deconstructed chicken
stew for neo-pragmatics

cannot sustain a poetics.
How one man, single-handed
killed an entire Venezuelan

badminton team, learn.
On your knees,

citizen.
Fervent
pastries.
Excessive
unity.
Racial

backgrounds?
Fatuous

coherence.
Social
problems

conceivable only
in poetic terms
of a jargonite
PhD&D.

Not our belief, our practice.
As in: "Through
the fires of
critical theory,
walk."

Clitoral studies.
Literally. His works,
insufficiently obscure,

were.

Joe Average.
Criminal Neglect
Against Humanity.

Woe is me.
Me is us.
Moe is We.
Cut into your right

to more free time. Armed.
At the popular level

action movie DVDs, Slavoj
Žižek on the special features.

Never writing a poem
not writing a poetry. Write
a reading. Design

a casino. Book
to museum

as poem

to cognitive frame.
Commonsense
and gravity
pull me to earth. Lovingly, He

marks you as territory, charms away
toothaches with a hurtin' song.

Realism as a *cause*?

Mating habits
of the Common Reader.
Traditionally empty

as statistics dream.

SNOWBALL IN HELL TURNS TO BILLIARD BALL

Startingplace, a commonplace. A hangaround, loiterature.

All art-making is epiphenomenal of the organisation of human society in and through and by language.

All art-making is epiphenomenal ~~of the~~ organisation of human society ~~in and through and~~ by language.

▼

"The snowball appears in Hell
every morning at seven." (G. Bowering)

▼

But what is poetry?

"It is not that the presence of poetic qualities compels a certain kind of attention but that the paying of a certain kind of attention results in the emergence of poetic qualities [...] definitions of poetry are recipes, for by directing readers as to what to look for in a poem, they instruct them in ways of looking that will produce what they expect to see." (S. Fish)

The poem, a thing of grammar, ideology, capitalism, feeling, an affective machine, an effective un-thing, best understood not as. A not-thing.

"What is a 'thing?' All is movement, a flowing." (K. Patchen). A poem. Poetry. Way. Of paying. Attention. Poetry. Is. A. Poetry is a way of paying attention.

Process. The effects of poetic qualities. Depth-effects. Effects of recognition. Poetic reading produces poetry. Poetry is effects of reading poetically.

In local atomic interpretative community coterie contexts, symbolic micro-economies, littlefields, moistlands, emergencies, readers highlight identify itemise specific functions, applications, iterations. Reader-reflective, recognition-effective. Poetic is custom to needs.

If a text feels like poetry it is poetry because you read it poetically it affects you as poetry it is poetry. Congratulations: found poetry. Gustave F. wrestled bears. "For is there not poetry everywhere – if it exists at all?" (G. Flaubert)

▼

Is that *stuff poetry?*

Pop fiction, movies, light non-fiction, Freeto Lay, mainly presume the consumer will ingest the product only once. First time. Full disclosure. Clear. Direct. Here-ism. Arresting an image in every line. Devastating a crunch in every bite.

But "a poetry collection is like a record collection." (R. Maurer)

Bafflement, puzzlement, difference, strangeness, unfamiliarity raise curiosity, invite long-term engagement. "Love don't come easy" (L. Dozier et al.). Poetry is not a consumable. "It's a game of give and take" (P. Collins). You can't hurry, so *DON'T RUSH*. Poetry is

a place in common, a conversation, not a referendum of *LIKE*.

Then what is culture?

Obviously Great Writings (*THE LITERARY CANON ETC.*) are, obviously, great because they obviously have the obvious character of Being Obviously Great. So: obvious.

Qualities of Obvious Greatness (non-exhaustively): atheism, bad taste, camp, circuitousness, contradiction, cruelty, despair, digression, dimness, dishonesty, disorder, dissonance, fascist cravings, flakiness, foolishness, horror, idiocy, illogic, incest, layaboutishness, lust, mental illness, misanthropy, obscurity, oppositionality, palimsestuousness, pettiness, polysemy, poly-vocality, pretentiousness, self-indulgence, sexual deviance, strangeness, stupidity, substance abuse, tonal discord, vegetativity, vengefulness, violence.

Culture is ordinary.

▼

And here you are, Reader, *enjoying culture.*

"Poetry's role remains primarily affective: *to joyfully render the present even more intolerable than it already is,* while gesturing toward new forms of affinity, agency, and association." (R. Farr)

If poetry's (needed) social role is disaffection, the poetry, contingently, is whatever feeling, vibe, bond, etc, people get from the idea that they are contemplating poetry. Try it. Poet, go out and Be Cultural. In listening to a poetry reading watching Cirque du Soleil in these dark days at least half the experience is "Hey, here I am listening to a poetry reading watching Cirque du Soleil in these dark days." The mediation of money, the financialisation of everyday life, makes the salutary Ordinary of art (everyday) ever more

remote.

The less ordinary the more special the less known except through the jellybean lens of Being Cultural.

So what kind of poetry is needed when not Being Cultural?

▼

What's needed.

You are never (not) alone. The house of language you live in. The result
of

social processes - non-individual - years - many thousands - telepathic
thought - continuous - direct connect with other

humans, animals.
Or literacy. Every book your reading
touches forms
your writing. The
archive - a literal(ly) later(ally) human community. An

inky pixelly pencilly bloody community of
kinships antagonisms sedimentations permissions poisons balms

mice and dusts; writes its books
through a grammatical (hands-on-the-joystick) collective
you. Books

are written by communities.

Now do you
recognise yourself in this text,
or how do

you? "The text that you write must prove to me that it desires me." (R.
Barthes)

Poetics of the astrology column. Mythopoetics. Poetics of rocks,
trees, rooks, lions. Poetics of the personal. "Personal emotion" – as in
"everybody's had one

emotion." Libidinal, narcissistic poetics. Confessionabsolution.

Deep into the reader's eyes. Meaningful coincidence. Synchronicity.

I-Ching. Karma as metaphysical recycling. Paranoia. The text the abyss

stares back, looking characteristically like Mona Lisa Great Composer. Stares back

because perception is animal and language is social.

Not self-recognition, but proto-semantic recognition of this "self" as discursively (socially) constituted. Recognition of the self as a subject constituted in language.

Not of person but of personhood. The text calls out. Pisces, your plan is unfolding. The commodity calls out. These boots were made to stand your hairbrush in. "Your (political) desires reflect back" – as in "constitutively."

Recognition-effects.

In the poetics of quietude, *recognition-effects* are craftily worked to produce: *accessibility,*

the effect of

▼

~~Orchestrate munchkin cushion pillowclouds of self-rec.~~

~~Aim well the politicoculturo venom-arrow of intent, Marxist hunter!~~

Cultivate an impossible relationship with language.

▼

IN: *Yeah, sure, all that – but can you light a match?*

OUT: I have in the past, and assume that I could again if called to in the future.

OUT: *Is the plastic cigarette lighter to gradeschool arson what the pocket calculator is to gradeschool arithmetic?*

IN: A single, well placed match could be forever.

▼

"I am the master of my fate:
I am the captain of my soul." (E. Henley)

"Maybe we'll leave come springtime
Meanwhile, have another beer." (D. Henley)

▼

Loiter on.
Criminal-
ly dialogic, misintend.

▼

In response to apparently abstract non-referential pre- or post-semiotic word-salad writing, sympathetic-antagonistic readers say they witness an authorial subjectivity leak out, in spite of the de-personalising (de-personality-ifying) procedure used to crank out such yarning text. A villainous heartless or disheartening (tear my quartz heart out method by method) intent is foiled by the glowing nebula of Human Spirit, shining through the formalist armour's chinks.

And so they are right. Human does prevail. Bright traces (misrecognised as authorial personality personhood quality) that are the very traces of the long term collective, evolutionary, human social process that *is* language, prevail.

"[Hugo Ball's] relapse to the rhythms of the [Catholic] mass in the middle of an outrageous Dadaist spectacle is not only funny; it is, like the sudden locating experience of Zanzibar, a reminder of how deeply constituted, socially, language always is, even when the decision has been made to abandon its identifiable semantic freight." (R. Williams)

The glow of personality or personhood (appears to) persist(s) because language is both socially constituted and humanly constituting. Animal and social, humans make language (as a process) and are made by language (as a process). As human, language always looks humane. Not personality, not individuality shining, but a collective, processual humanness called language. That common place: you (again).

▼

But does a neologism announce a nonce?

Risqué nonce-words refer to "words" as category and abstract concept. As a discursive *event*. Nonce words look thingy a moment, until one remembers events are time, process, not things. Psych-out non-words that will could have been functional (= actual) words. Quote you a "moeys," raise you a "llud" (p.inman). Nonce is an un-concept or not-concept, non-concept. Noncept. Wordness performed, empty but of the concept of word. Wordness performed, stripped. Nuditives, if you will. Syntax uncloaked as a system to learn or learn to beat.

Pay you a gold *Louis C.*: "The nonce-word undermines the entire procedure socializing the word as such."

So you think you can coin? Neologisms coin concepts. Accrue value, aspiring to be another actual (=functional) word. Non-counterfeit, a 24k neologism leaves the writer's quill spent, is spent, enters discursive circulation. New logos. Current currency.

nonce word versus *neologism*. Nonce is (usually) used only once. Ammunitive. Noncept. Not a coinage. Neologism is a new silver dollar in the realm. Rechargeable value. Neologist: writer as name-maker. I am a writer, my job is to name. Noncers quit that job, gone into lumpen unprofessionality. Coiners hold out for the pension, maximal returns.

"is 'oneitd'
a word? to be done
[what] with the nonce
word." (L. Cabri)

Then who's the fastest pun in the West?

Degrees of categorical separation. Puns facilitate knowledge, puns are
the toenail oil, the sweaty palm-butter of verbal thought-machine. From
pun to pun, side-step to side-step, any object can gang up with any
other. Unlimited limits (semiosis). Lightning grease. Language a vineous
or rhizomatic punkin patch. Crime and punishment need a good de-
fence. *Who's talking shit about the pun?*

More cats than you could fit in a puncheon. From pun one: *punt* → a
complex religious symbol → an item of secular economic exchange →
something harvested under conditions of exploitation → something
that puts vitamins into bodies → a carrier of seed to propagate a species
→ something that may have travelled 2000 miles or years → fruit base
of an intoxicant that stains beige or paler pants → purple or greenish
spheroid → [*Etcetera.*] Just a (humble punlet of a) grape, or perhaps a
punitive, angry chimera. Cut, crushed, squeezed. A bootless ceremony
of punletting. *Hands off the pun.*

Not funny. As the doubling of meaning, the contingency of meaning,
the piercing punctum of the pun-jab brings into the body's awareness
the unity, arbitrariness, unsystematic social complexity of language.
Always teetering over a puntrap, never punless. Relational meaning,
meaning *meaning* at its fullest and fowlest, aloft. It is de-meaning to
devalue the pun. *Drop the pun or I'll shoot.*

Puns the doubling tripling quadrupling of ref. Cents sense. Poets are
value-maximizers in language. Thumb and forefinger of a hoarding poet,
a punnypincher.

Taken far enough to become the basis of a poetics, this glibly rational,
chaste activity of punnigrammatical, categorical punnology – name

proliferation, categorical side-step, tic-tac-2pac-toe square dancing –
heats dancers' brains to hyper-rationality, to burst.

Punctilious yet punch-drunk, the pun wines blood.

▼

Some call them theoretical concerns. Concerns, like background of a
portrait. Concerns, where lines converge. Wall / slash / ceiling.

Or concerns as afterimages, viewable in playback after race to page's end.
Not a concern.

Concerns, some call them theoretical, are poem-co-extensive.
Indistinguishable. Not behind, peekaboo. Not driving. Not impelling,
whip-smart crazy-poem. Not a semantic engine, horsepower. Not
feeding, horsemeat for (lateral argument) critical meatloaf.

Theoretical concerns are not the work's secret. Secrets are not poetry's
concern.

A constant overflow, irrepressible excess of – fuse of signification itself –
meaning undermines the message. Any message a poem could pony-run
on.

I mean, *can you fit a mattress in your earhole?*

I mean, that quote you may know – "I think it has an orange bed in
it, more than the ear can hold" (F. O'Hara) – stuffing, springs – *that*
concerns poetry.

▼

Where are the springs of poetry?

Somewhere, later, in the metaphor. Be like a gazelle on the mountains of
spices. Squish the grapes of wrath. Meaning emerges in the gap between

terms as poles. But in these gaps, as the light liquid significance breaks from the ideobulb, facilitating legibility (it was so dry dark before), inevitable losses / slash / excesses accrue. Parentless remnants remain.

If such loss / slash / excess always attends metaphor, such loss always attends; it is not merely a kind of leak when, for example, Rabelais' French renders into Kutenai (Ktunaxa).

"The movement to resemblance effects an escape of difference, yet there is always an irreducible, unmasterable remnant in the figure that is neither resemblance nor difference but the indeterminacy of both." (S. McCaffery)

Sensing loss, does (aesthetic) conscience:
1 - drive you to mend the leaks, to recuperate the remnants
2 - drive you around the turnpikes (Paterson, New Jersey) of unlimited semiosis
3 - drive you to give up poetry by silence and slash or slash suicide

Too often, (1). Writing craft is too often too (1). Shut the windows, keep out the drafts. Cold-shoulder contingency out of the word. Close chinks in a cultural armour. Violent subjugation of material. (1)'s a desire to exterminate semiotic orphans, made by aesthetic conscience into a grim, glorious duty. Consequently, too often the (1) (2) road ends at (3).

▼

the pizza effect. By which a mediocre, bready recipe becomes more popular outside of Italy than inside, causing the recipe to eventually become a cultural keynote at festivals of the Italian within and without the boot. (Also known as *culinary blow-back*.)

the [johann sebastian] bach effect. By which a certain idiosyncratic counterpoint of a long maligned composer becomes institutionalised as the exact practical definition of good counterpoint against which other counterpoints become incorrect or idiosyncratic. (Also known as *the*

34

institutional construction of Quality.)

▼

Avant-Garde®. Social movements retro-fitted as mere style. Techniques and devices as neat-o discursive gadgets. Experimentalism as pop culture. Sound poetry as kitsch. The Antonin Artaud Lookalike Contest Theatre of Wild Wicked Wacky. Cult of the enthusigasm.

▼
▼
▼
▼
▼

►►►►►►►►►► Press-
     -ed by (my) be-
     -lated-
     -ness to-
     -wards socio-
     -logy.

Did I keep you waiting long?

Belatedness (I mean you and I, Reader) poses problems. Familiar.

Where doth slice the cutting edge? (Don't matter.) *Where is the battle line hot?* (All's cool.) *Pounce on evercreeping Next Thing?* (Non.) *Restage reconstruct familiar unfamiliar?* (No.) *Neo-aestheticise anti-aesthetic as History is Awesome?* (Rather jump to cloud **nein**.)

From a situation in which everything is possible, suddenly nothing can happen.

To stay sharp ignited first-wave blade, keep critically noserash close to coticule whetstone theory-grind touchscreen. That is, keep rethinking problems, not restaging vintage solutions.

This is poetry. Today.
Do you have a *problem* with that, buddy?
You should, my friend, *have a problem.*

So what's your problem?
Reader? Poet?

This. Imperative.

From a situation in which anything is possible, suddenly nothing can happen (again).

▼

Who isn't complicit?

Complicity is not a line to draw. It is a condition to be negotiated. Attended on multiple levels. Where. When. How.

What looks like conscious consent is (but) marginally conscious. True also of intent. Marginally rational.

What kind of unconscious underlies unconscious irrational complicity?
Rather than a shadow well of the repressed wherefrom to draw inky buckets of phantasy, a pragmatic political unconscious. A strata of mind that accumulates ideological. Sediment. Silently.

Is that a river or a lake?
A mouth?
Onslaught?
An unsystem?
A watery commonplace?

Quietly masticating issues the conscious mind lacks language to taste. Thousand and one stomachs of the political unconscious.

▼

"Ideas don't come without limbs, and so these are no longer ideas but limbs, limbs fighting among themselves.

The mental world was never anything but that which remains from a hellish trampling of organs." (A. Artaud)

▼

Do you enjoy writing?

In panic? Writing today is a perfectlittlehellride in a skullshape. When nothing can happen, everything is at [the] stake.

Any poetics today bears – mist – the weight of history, horror of contemporaneity. Lightly, heavily, unbearably. *Trapped in a capitalist Hellucinatio; the world.* "Le monde n'est qu'abusion." (F. Villon) No aesthetic retreat, no formalist refuge. None. So, know what you bear. And how do you bear it.

So. Everything that could be learned. Everything that could be done. All the possible failures. Futures. All the potential meanings. Each path. "All the flux, all the rays." (A. Césaire) The harm you're sure to do.

And so. Every saying. Every story. Every essay. Borne down upon. Every poem the first-last. "Everything is summoned. Everything awaits." (Ibid.)

Enjoy writing?

"We are using our own skins for wallpaper and we cannot win." (J. Berryman)

▼

"the Gothic novel displays 'the inevitable fruits of the revolutionary

shocks felt by all of Europe [...] For those who know all the miseries
with which scoundrels can oppress [...] the novel became as difficult to
write as it was monotonous to read. [...] It was necessary to call Hell to
the rescue..." (Sade)

▼

"No place for beginners or sensitive hearts
When sentiment is left to chance
No place to be ending but somewhere to start
No need to ask" (Sade)

▼

Terms misappropriated from S. Ngai: *stuplimity*; *the stuplime*. Stupid +
sublime. *Sublimely stupid?* No: a junked-up, urine-stained, mushrumpsy
sublime plus/minus uncanny stupid. A great blue arc volting between
ideational poles. Dangerous current from demonically complex to
grimly idiotic.

Stuplime produces macro micro electro sensations electifications, dense
disharmonious cultural frequencies. In stuplimity. Torrent of dissonant
signals somewhere between nearly and totally impossible to recuperate.
Where to sit? Which direction to face? Where to put it?

Remember little Regan, invaded in her cute soul, possessed, yes, friends,
impassioned, Reader, by Mr. Howdy. The music. Expensive toys (mom
is so rich – she's an actress!) and 45 rpm singles – probably K-C and the
Sunshine Band – flying across, whirling around, her room. She has her
back stage-forward. Now she turns to address addressees. Being rigorous
but not rigid, poetic not scientific, turns not her body, turns only her
ventriloquesque head 180°.

Simultaneously: back to audience, face to audience. In the voice – she
speaks the voices of the so many in so many voices – of one who may as

well have been Dudley Moore, a director who makes films about student protest American politics Boston as Berkeley who had his own stiff neck broken trying the same damned trick, Regan says in the third person: *Do you know what she did, your c**nting daughter?*

Counting daughter – to say *divisive*. Some of the addressees vomit. Some run out of the theatre. Some of the addressees howl. Some scream. Some of the addressees wonder how. Some threaten. Some pray to. Some roll. Many laugh – but the laughter's funnee. In her culturally saturated little bedroom, Regan Howdy's is the address-reception-address of the *stuplime*.

▼

Is poetry undead?

Poetry is not dead. The term *poetry* is not dead. Poetry, the term, balloon, collapses. To supernova. *What structural role do supernovae play?*

Poetry is alive. Whatever falls outside the gamesmanship of type: call it poetry. Lineated fictions with feelings, birds, rocks, trees, badgers, canoes, earth: call it poetry. Rhyming doggerel for an open mic funeral wedding memorial rally: call it poetry. Versified absolutist propaganda: call it poetry. Pasta-machine experimentalism (i.e. churn hip discourse through procedure): call it poetry. Non-honorific, the term glows more alive.

Poetry is dead. Vulture's eye view sees poetry pluralised too far, carnage of poetical body fragments strewn. Projecting from the particular universal: only *this* particular poetry eats the universal early worm. Only *this* poetry lives. Everything else is not poetry. Poetry dies. Poetry is dead. Delicious stink critical repast.

Yes, poetry is dead. Certain poetry is dead (for now). Dead things feed living things. Re-past. Poetry can no longer rely for its wages' nutrition on old claims old voices old foes old ancientness. If poetry would cleave mightily to ancientness, poetry has to go angel ahead looking backwards, as if early middle late long twentieth century never began-ended. Go ahead, call it poetry. Call it certain poetry. Just one of the living poetries, throbbing through every everyday. Like it or don't.

No, poetry is not dead. Certainly not dead. Confident declarations of cultural deaths are the grace a vulture says at table. *Prayers to other vultures? Nekhebet?* Headlines in a crowded graveyard. The dead return through the living. As long as libraries books archives language exist, the possibility of encounter remains. Poetry won't die. Poetry won't die as long as the reading of poetry is possible. As long as such loitering attention can be paid.

Just so. "I saw dead things engender life, and the dead were consumed by the breath of life." (Alcuin of York)

Poetry cannot die.

BIWRIXLE

llama w
ill voluntar
ism leg
less force squirrel-
wing membr

ane elegy d
irge win
ce pagan pop
pies burning
over green skull-li
ke cabbages black

mounds li
fe of vegetables' lea
ves bore in
bearded development all

ege the natur
naturalists colour-f
leck tractor ray
ces illusions light

silk slippers dus
ty city clogs, hooflike
watermelon cleft empty

ness of state

twitter boi
l mutter whist
le trout tit ill
ate glass gerund
dive horseback pelt
anteater-ton
gue blown crystal

line theatre chir
ring bourgeois toa
d add quarrel dye t
o slopes crisp t
toast crunch root
s at gold cognac, ant

hology jangle keys
of language t
hick-walle
d semivowel abyss
ticklish request en
crust de
vout fat talk with
lactifluous competence

thesis tail cof
fee nupt
ial acci

dent omelette
immense lottery wheel

whirr hypo-
critical acorns mon
k's cap antennae
ar is
ta te
got
hic pine

cone smelt milk
lancet tel
egram yacht collusio
n dry telephone drip…
drip…drip…

drip… small-c
small-com
modity belt be
littling shuttlecock apple
told listen
ed understood

icy spa
zz swans m
ini squints h

ue-noise jaguar

's ear flau
tist lip oilsick c

anti allprize
coal strawberries
cochineal bead ver
million lump

damp chemise rot to ope
n velvet azure
ibsen problem sum
mon burnoose zouave a
barber shaving the bürgermeister

grazes! and if pa
le dim
innuendo in
fidel wrinkles raise
vision-teeth
crushed by binoculars cr
umble pol
icemanly phizz je
suitical tentacle
caresses con

vexity frisky
didactic bi
foliate
pleophonous

whirlw
ind pool incunabular sur
f well-m
eant alcazarian inte

rjections: forward!

lower!

away!

tap!

cameo!

enough!

enough!

INTROSPECTIVE DATA

Remember to be more guarded in the beginning and more gradually to disclose what is to be clarified here.
                        –Marquis de Sade

La résponse est le malheur de la question.
                        –Maurice Blanchot

What is the structure of the question?

"What we knew when we were you know where?" (S. Rodefer)

Do you like beautiful poetry?

What if reality gets in the way?

Normalcy is pathological?

Discord, variance, debts, divisions, murmurs, and sedition?

Who could have written this?

"Who promises the food?" (A. Notley)

How many definitions of *HUMANISM* can you fit
1 - into a telephone booth
2 - onto a 1-gigabyte flash drive

Everything is interesting?
Portable hole?

Massacre at The Philosopher's Café?

I was so turned around I believed
....
That wheat flour was potash
And a mortar a felt hat

....
That the sky was a copper pan
And clouds were calf-skins
That the morning was evening
And a cabbage stump a turnip
The soured beer was young wine
And a battering ram a windmill
And a hangman's noose a bridle
                        —F. Villon

Which would be worse
1 - the end of the world
2 - continuation of the world as is

Which of the following is most likely
1 - the end of the world
2 - the end of capitalism

Should people
1 - stop complaining
2 - complain better

When did despair become mainstream?

"Can feelings have a history?" (B. Geremek)

How do you know when an event is over?

Line in the sand or lying in the sand?

Has science caught up with Marxism?

Are you surprised?

Is it a sign of something bad or is it a bad sign?

July 3. We breakfasted off fried crayfish patties and indescribable coffee. While the others were busy with the loading and oiling and gassing, I heated a silver dollar and wrapped it carefully in my muffler; then, when we were all in the car, the trailer chain examined and in order, I tossed the hot coin to our host, the scaly innkeeper. His roar of pain and rage was music to my ears.
                                                        –K. Patchen

Do you have any questions about money?

What austerity measures are you taking?

How do you explain the value of $1,000,000,000,000?

To a six-year old?

Do you envision the globalised economy as
1 - a spider's web
2 - microorganisms at play in a drop of saliva
3 - plumbing
4 - a network of highways
5 - a crimson blob

When do you expect your current job to end?

Does the BOTTOM LINE evoke
1 - a guillotine
2 - longhand division
3 - a tan line

What is the function of the shoestring in a SHOESTRING BUDGET?

The science of ECONOMICS is most like
1 - phrenology
2 - astrology
3 - dianetics
4 - remote viewing
5 - divination by disembowelment

What form of privation makes you feel most virtuous?

Do you deserve to be rich?

When something costs AN ARM AND A LEG must the limbs you pay with be your own?

Is the moral character of wealth
1 - its use
2 - its possession
3 - its accumulation
4 - its invisible hand

"How do ghosts become obese?" (S. Dali)

> *Children, go and play in the park, and take care while admiring the*
> *swans swimming not to fall into the ornamental lake.*
> —Lautréamont

Which consumer commodity best defines your generation?

Pawnshop – as explanatory trope?

Is a user
1 - ON the internet (when at work)
2 - AT the internet (when at play)
3 - IN the internet (when depressed)

"Who in a place of amusement is really being amused?" (A. Huxley)

Just as people grow to resemble their electronic devices?

Is the content of *UTOPIA*
1 - happiness
2 - fulfillment
3 - immortality
4 - meaning
5 - justice

Are your hopes practical, specific or general?

Do you bear traces of the effort to raise yourself?

Would you marry a social climber?

Does the boss have a gender?

Do you feel cheated that your career might be cut short by an environmental apocalypse?

Push it to the crisis – or let the moment ripen?

Revolutionary patience?

Anyone can see that a pretty face is pretty, but how can one know
how pretty it really is until its worth has been awarded a diploma?
—N. Chernychevsky

Spoiled ballot in a beauty contest?

Is a HALF-BAKED idea undercooked
1 - ceramic
2 - bread
3 - pastry
4 - lasagna

Did you stop paying attention after the climax or in spite of the climax?

Is this sticky crap on the floor part of the spectacle?

Do you have a close friend whose art you actively dislike?

Dry-entry funk and/or white jazz?

Would you have sex with a bad artist?

Art-positive or art-negative?

Aesthetic immanence or depleted uranium?

I happened on a painter yesternight,
The only cunning man in Christendom,
For he can temper poison with his oil
That whoso looks upon the work he draws
Shall, with the beams that issue from his sight,
Suck venom to his breast and slay himself.
                    —Anonymous, *Arden of Faversham*

Which is most obscene
1 - pornography
2 - real estate
3 - conceptual art

Are landlords socially necessary?

Is GROWTH
1 - cancerous
2 - arboreal
3 - mycelian

When you think of MAKING ENDS MEET, is the cord
1 - twine
2 - live wire
3 - rope
4 - chain

Easy as pissing your pants?

"What would have led us to consider and regard the world as
reasonable?" (M. Foucault)

Revolution is
1 - a joke
2 - a disaster
3 - a necessity

Would you like the dick-all sandwich or the all-dick sandwich?

On Tuesday May 10, 2011 an 'unidentified Asian man jumped to his death [...] from the 147th floor of Dubai's Burj Khalifa, the world's tallest building, slamming into a terrace 39 floors below [...] Local reports said the man, believed to be in his 30s, became the first to commit suicide from the 160 storey building, which broke engineering and architectural records when it opened in January 2010.'

According to The National newspaper, the man 'had asked for a holiday and been denied it.'

In what part of your body do you carry your grief?

Is there room for everyone to succeed?

When you hear someone BURNED A BRIDGE, is the burnt bridge
1 - ahead
2 - behind

Is your life going well?

When you hear the word LOSER who comes to mind?

Is this person a LOSER
1 - AT capitalism
2 - IN capitalism
3 - OF capitalism
4 - TO capitalism

When you call someone a PRICK, do you imagine
1 - an action
2 - an encounter
3 - a protrusion

When you suffer a *PAIN IN THE ASS* is the pain
1 - in the buttocks
2 - in the rectum

When you grant a favour, do you expect
1 - a reciprocal favour
2 - gratitude
3 - friendship
4 - love

Do you trust a person who wants to be liked by everyone?

Can you tell it's a smile from this angle?

Real accident fake blood?

Will your funeral be well-attended?

Why weren't you popular in high school?

Is the perfect crime unpunished or undiscovered?

A Board of Directors with jet-packs?

Is it possible to design a punishment commensurate with the crime?

If *YES* to the above, is it possible to execute that punishment?

What if they'd just amputated his thumbs at birth?

Are you a good person?

Two years later a search-party had found them, hobbling along [through the jungle] on improvised crutches, toothless and suffering from half-healed fractures. It seems there was no calcium in the area. Chickens couldn't lay eggs, there was nothing to form the shell. Cows gave milk, but it was watery and translucent, with no calcium in it.
                                                              —W.S. Burroughs

Are wages adequate compensation for life spent at work?

Is human labour
1 - purchased
2 - extracted
3 - its own reward

Which of the following is a luxury
1 - leisure time
2 - inebriants (alcohol, soft drugs)
3 - jewellery

Do you work harder than your friends?

Is the DROP IN A BUCKET
1 - milk from a goat's udder
2 - rain from a leaky ceiling
3 - coin from an almsgiver's pocket

Are you tired emotionally, mentally or physically?

How long can I live on apples and bourbon?

Is foxglove edible?

At what point does sleeping-in become immodest?
1 - 10:30 am
2 - 12:00 pm
3 - 3:00 pm

4 - 5:00 pm

At what point does it become immoral?

If it's not WHITE GUILT, what could it be?

Is a coma like a long nap?

Is the position that radical social change is impossible a radical position?

Indifference, apathy or accommodation?

Disaffection, contempt, outrage or resentment?

Should a gob of spit include phlegm?

Embrace. *Negativity.*

Hope. Keeps. You. *Down.*

Wish. You. A. Deep. *Ambivalence.*

Resist. Compulsory. *Optimism.*

Would. Rather. *Not.*

My. *Oui.* Says. *Non.*

Dedescribed.

Devoked.

Defeatured.

Decreated.

Don't. Say. *Nothing.*

If. You. Can. *Can't.* You. Will. *Never.*

Smells like wood like oil paint in the garret. Like baby flesh paint.
The babytree is in bloom. Babies have blossomed on it from the
beginning and forever. Rosy twilight. Babies withering ripening
rotting on them. On the babytree ... The rustling babies.
                                        –U. Allemann

How many times did you hear the word LOVE today?

Does the word LOVE
1 - give solace
2 - induce panic

Do you consult pop songs for relationship advice?

Have you ever been sexually happy?

Are you sexually attracted to happiness?

Would you have a child with an abortionist?
Are babies predominantly
1 - repulsive
2 - adorable

Do you patrol the boundaries of your sexual orientation
1 - in a jeep
2 - on a dromedary
3 - stopping by woods on a snowy evening

When did tattoos, piercings and funky facial hair become the new
power suit?

If the proposed *minimum wage* rise amounts to less than half the
accepted *living wage*, is that *IRONY*?

Can you fight off a rapist ironically?

Can you revolt ironically?

Have you experienced love as self-hatred?

Who stuffed wet chewing tobacco into the top of my snorkel?

Do you know your way around the bottom of the lake?

Does your given name suit you?

Have you ever pretended you don't speak English?

Would you have chosen to be born?

                                        shuck my responsibilities for
                                          shirk my responsibilities

wholesome slaughter for
wholesale slaughter

the blind elephant for
the whole elephant

i urge you not to for
i forbid you to

personal banger for
personal banker

cast in cement for
set in stone

third bicycle for
third policeman

fire exchange for
fire escape

intersection for
intercourse

chevrolet for
beaujolais

lovestyle for
lifestyle

sadness for
sardines

empathy for
apathy

adopt for

avoid

for for
against

library of progress for
library of congress

count lucky stars for
thank lucky stars

rulitary millers for
military rulers

prince of peach for
prince of peace

settled with for
saddled with

mendicant for
medicine

penny up for
pony up

it will all wash out in the laundry for
it will all come out in the wash

surgical guts for
surgical cuts

human mirror for
human microphone

perplexion for
condition

oil witch for
oil rich

fun razor for
fundraiser

grease for
grief

NAFTA for
NATO

Spaniard in the works for
spanner in the works

lose my temperature for
lose my temper

anachronists for
anarchists

ground zero for
clean slate

rockwilder for
rotwiler

city long for
city wide

peasants for
pedants

long for
back

Have fat people lost control of their lives?

How often do you wish your body were different?

Are your friends better looking than you are?

Why look tough?

Is sincerity a strength or a liability?

On whose terms?

New master narrative as
1 - adaptation
2 - remake
3 - reboot
4 - clone

Can an ideology be plagiarised?

Do competitive hot-dog eaters race themselves, each other or a clock?

Is the BIOLOGICAL CLOCK wired to an alarm or an explosive?

History – first draft or final proofing?

Time measured in burnt animal fats?

What is your favourite twentieth century invention?

"Can hope be disappointed?" (E. Bloch)

Have they thrown away the last disposable camera?

> *The moment's shortened – but not the ear*
> *the heart in panic pants*
> *the minute splits, and swarms apart*
> *a thousand agitated ants.*
> —Z. Zelk

Are bananas produced using slave labour considered vegan?

Is veganism an eating disorder?

Are vegans a cult?

Eating fast-food in a crowded elevator?

Is it morally worse to murder
1 - a fresh newborn
2 - an accomplished senior

Are switchblades still illegal?

Glazed, glassy, glass, or vile jelly?

Are people with pets
1 - owners
2 - masters
3 - protectors

FREE AS A BIRD to fight for food, territory or sex?

Does the talking hyena indicate that it's "just a story"?

NEOLIBERAL WEREWOLFISM?

Do you imagine your body being eaten?

What brand of cologne do necrobobsledders wear?

Ketchup fortune?

Does burning flesh smell like roast meat?

> *With third-rate meat*
> *let's get rid of*
> *the* **rats** *of* **the unconditioned**
>
> *who have never felt*
> ....
>
> *the imposition of the outside which sleeps,*
> *like an inside, burst from the latrines*
> *of the canal where we shit death*
> — A. Artaud

"God or phosphenes?" (C. Smith)

Scream, cry, *then* puke?

Between coughs, sneezes or seizures?

If you could have only one nightmare, which would it be?

An insanity like flypaper?

Is suicide
1 - bold
2 - desperate
3 - murder

Will the afterlife be more like an airport or a casino?

Will the angels of Heaven carry trumpets of
1 - gold
2 - brass
3 - chrome
4 - nanofibre

Is *HUMAN SPIRIT*
1 - congealed blood
2 - a gas
3 - a fluid
4 - an energy

What does laughter mean
1 - from the podium
2 - in solitary confinement
3 - on a deathbed
4 - as sea levels rise

Can you fake laughter convincingly?

Grins, bared teeth, or asemic grunts?

The Yeomanry had dismounted – some were easing their horse's girth, others adjusting their accoutrements, and some were wiping their sabres. Several mounds of human beings still remained where they had fallen, crushed down and smothered. Some were still groaning, others with staring eyes, were gasping for breath and others would never breathe no more. All was silent save those low sounds, and the occasional snorting and pawing of the steeds.
—S. Bamford

Are you a victim or are you a survivor?

What do abuser and victim share?

Is the IRON FIST a prosthetic?

Are the cops in your city middle class or lower class?

Is someone WHIP-SMART
1 - smart as a whip
2 - trained to pain

Is torture a collaborative activity?

Is it a FIGHT if one party doesn't resist?

If ownership rights don't include your genes, do they include your traumas?

Still lonely?

Sugary surgery?

Is anything bothering you?

Why did I have to see that?

We must learn more of the fated, fearful process of thought which makes people feel not only justified, but that they have a duty to destroy others.

—W. Soyinka

What is your favourite racist joke?

Would you rename Thanksgiving Day GENOCIDE DAY?

"Does Martin Luther King Day constitute the real killing of Martin Luther King?"(N. Smith)

When you sing along with your favourite gangster rap, do you say the N-word?

Is contemplative disinterest
1 - baleful
2 - salutary

Witness – to whiteness?

Mayonnaise – as a binding agent?

Have you ever experienced a patriotic sentiment?

If YES to the above, were you
1 - in a public washroom
2 - watching television
3 - talking intimately with the Other

Canadians will elect a First Nations Prime Minister
1 - in 25 years
2 - in 10 years
3 - ∞

If 1 or 2 of the above, which party will the new PM belong to?

Sequel to a massacre or resumption of a massacre?

When something is HARD TO SWALLOW, is the difficulty
1 - flavour
2 - texture
3 - size

> *Today it is impossible to say for certain why people are punished: all concepts in which an entire process is semiotically concentrated elude definition; only that which has no history is definable.*
> —F. Nietzsche

Are there certain words you know you don't understand?

Are there certain words you think everyone else uses incorrectly?

How do words become opaque?

Antonymic synonym?

Interrogative metonym?

Pleonasms induce memory loss?

Tragic *cum* abject?

No pun intended, none taken?

Abstraction or euphemism (for security purposes)?

Gallows, galley or gall?

Disinterested to uninterested?

Rigged, loaded or cocked?

Time measured in de-accessioned books?

Wikipedia print-edition?

Did you used to know or expect to find out?

> *The louse on Stilitano's collar, still invisible to the other men,*
> *was not a small stray spot; it was moving; it shifted about with*
> *disturbing velocity, as if crossing and measuring its domain – its*
> *space rather. But it was not only at home; on Stilitano's collar it*
> *was the sign that he belonged to an unmistakably verminous world,*
> *despite his eau de cologne and silk shirt.*
> —J. Genet

How severely do panhandlers annoy you?

Do your politics exempt you from giving spare change?

Would you report SUSPICIOUS ACTIVITY?

"What kind of life must one have had to use the phrase HUMAN
GARBAGE?" (L. Boldt)

Have you ever been chased by police through a ballet studio?

You can guess most about a person's politics by
1 - postal code
2 - browser cache
3 - diet
4 - ethnicity

Has your front door ever been kicked in?

Were you at home at the time?

If you have the facts do you need a theory?

Is information knowledge?

A body count – without fractions?

Join or die?

Does truth presuppose falsehood?

Would you ever use the phrase *OF COURSE*?

Bolts. of. Annihilation.

Am. I. Yuppie. Scum?

Beauty. is. a. Consensual. Power.

Success. Ruins.

You. Might. Also. Enjoy.

Too. Busy. to. Cook?

Will. Have. Had. a. Long. Day.

Who. Eats. Who. Starves.

Rock. the. Boat. Not. the. Cradle.

Positivity. Is. Compliance. *Spiritualised.*

My nipples are dying for what happens most of the time. They're not as long as some I've seen, my nipples' form in regular space. Sweeten them, honey. My nipples are not claiming everything's the same, but they're staring at the screen thinking of you.
–D. Bellamy

Does poetry
1 - affirm the world as is
2 - improve the world
3 - do no work in the world
4 - beautify capitalism
5 - manipulate, confuse, obfuscate

"Does shame bring out the worst in narcissists?" (B.J. Bushman)

Which Canadian poet should definitely not be on a Canadian banknote?

$5, $20 or $1000?

Does applause smother art?

Would you like to author a cliché?

Does conceptual art provoke
1 - your contempt
2 - your hatred
3 - your envy

What does this line separate?

Is culture today
1 - a disorienting fragmentation
2 - an oppressive unity

Can someone like an artwork for the wrong reasons?

Why paint a canvas of an attacking grizzly bear?

When is a staple gun better used as a weapon?

Which song sums it all up?

Inaccurate mirror?

Time measured in diminishing royalty cheques?

Is it more musical to burn a munitions plant or bomb a concert hall?

Could a historiographer drive on his history, as a muleteer drives on his mule, – straight forward; ... [with all the] various

Accounts to reconcile:
Anecdotes to pick up:
Inscriptions to make out:
Stories to weave in:
Traditions to sift:
Personages to call upon:
Panygericks to paste up at this door:
Pasquinades at that:–

–L. Sterne

Is it quiet where you currently are?

Are you seated or standing?

Is there a payphone around here?

Where can I plug this in?

"What is literature thinking about?" (P. Macherey)

Why is there a grey school bus parked in front of this building?

Turkey sandwich or the concept of entropy?

Life, Total, Just Right or *Count Chocula*?

Who put blood puddings and sour cream in the bel of my tenor saxophone?

Should charitable book donation bins be filled with copies of *The Communist Manifesto*?

I'm going to have to ask: Is this leading up to a question?

74

If you didn't expect the Spanish Inquisition, did you expect the Fire Department?

Choose one
1 - Louise Bourgeois *fat with integrity*
2 - Twisted Sister *Stay Hungry*
3 - ●

> *when you have lost it all, everything to be said*
> *has been said*
> *I put my ear against the wall*
> *and listen to the slow*
> *erosion of concrete*
> *everybody is building shelters and vaults*
>   —P. Saarikoski

LAUGH PARTICLES

heh huh •hh
            huh huh heh heh hnh (.)•uhhh
uhhh huh huh ∘huh∘
•h
huh huh I had to st<u>o</u>p. ∘huh-huh∘ •e<u>u</u>h
That's h<u>o</u>rri:d. huh hu-hih ∘hh∘
                HA<u>A</u> ↑HA<u>A</u> Haa
H A <u>h</u> <u>a</u> ha ha ha •<u>uhh</u> •uhh
=hh hih heh heh ∘huh huh∘=
                    eh↑<u>hih</u> hih
hn ↑hn hn •hhh
heh heh (.) HUH-HAH! (.) ↑HAH
HAH HAH   HAH   HUH   HUH
        ih-hih
∘↑h<u>e</u>h huh •<u>hh</u> PLAYN(h)W(h)IZ O(h)R'N ya:h I thought∘
the same hhh!   heh-heh-heh-heh
hheh   heh
        hhhh<u>heh</u>-heh-heh
instihhhks of
            fhhhh
•hh hh   ehhhh
        <u>aaahhh</u>!
        hhhahahaha
the <u>li</u>ddle things, hhhHA HA   HA HA
                        heh heh heh
she hunts to (h) huh ↑huh ↑huh?

        <u>hhh</u>   ehh   eh   uh=
<u>h</u>eu:rtchise(h)e(h) If (or someth' •hh)
En here c<u>o</u>mes this ↑g<u>u</u>(h)u(h)<u>y</u>,
uh huh huh huh huuh
Um-hm.
(0.4) hunh-hunh-hunh hunh-hunh! Ye-hunh-hunh
                    Now yuh can tell'er
-hungh-hunh. •h!
•hh!
I have <u>no</u> idea <u>rilly</u> I (been) heh heh heh
=I'm'nna go r-r<u>a</u>:n now. ∘hu-hh-hh∘
'm 'nna go ra:n.
                 <u>n</u>h ha ↑ha h<u>a</u> ha.=
An th<u>e</u>n I'm go::un to a movie. ∘hh hh∘
(.)
                        eh ↑h<u>ih</u> hih hn ↑hn hn •hhh
•hhhh <u>I</u> don't no no or<u>i</u>ginal nickel.
(.)
I've I've stopped crying uhheh-heh-<u>heh</u>-heh-heh,
=home as well. •hh And then the
•hh And basically the only time that I hear
Hhhh uh huh
£It's not much. £•hhhh heh hhh
so: (.) petrified ((laughs))
Well not that's a pro↓f<u>ou</u>(hh)nd ↓st<u>a</u>(h)temen(hh)
We(hh)ll(.)
hu huh •hh hh=<u>Why:</u>
Eoh hh!
=h<u>uh</u> hh   •hhh

(h)you doh huh huh-   uh.

Looks like it's uh(h)↑on th(h) ↑'ott(h)om huh hih (.) shoo(h)oo

•↑e<u>hh</u> (.) huh <u>huh</u> huh <u>huh</u> huh <u>huh</u>

•e<u>hh</u> (.)

•ehh (.) huh ↑huh ↑huh ↑huh (.) huh huh huh huh

hah hah huh huh huh huh (.)

•↑ehh •↑<u>huh</u>=

u<u>hh</u>!

ehh h<u>e</u>h h<u>e</u>h h<u>e</u>h h<u>e</u>h heh

        heh heh heh heh (heh heh)

=eh h<u>u</u>h huh ↑hah hah

((chair creaks))

=•<u>e</u>hh

    hu-

=HA! uh HAH   •<u>e</u>h-uh

   HAH!   <u>HAT!</u>   BEF<u>O</u>RE.=

=AH H<u>A</u>H! HAH! HAH!

            ↑h<u>u</u>h! h<u>u</u>h! (.) hah hah huh

                eh heh! heh! heh! heh!=

heh h<u>a</u>h h<u>a</u>h

•<u>euhhh</u>

= (   ) Ha:t before.

        ↑u:::::::::h

=hoh-hoh ↑hoh-hoh hoh-hoh.

        •<u>euhh</u>- •<u>euhhh</u> •ehhh

u↑<u>AA:H</u> H<u>UH</u>- HAH H<u>UH</u>-HEUH

heuh-↑huh

    ehh h<u>i</u>h-h<u>i</u>h-h<u>i</u>h-h<u>i</u>h- heh h<u>e</u>uh=

        <u>eeh-euhh ↑hh?</u>

=he: ::h

     •∘ehh∘

uhh- huh-   huh

   ↑(Mym)y-   huh-huh

          a:h huh- ↑hah-huh

∘euh-huh • ehhh∘

Ye:h.

   Yhh e(h)eh

     heh heh heh heh heh- ↑eh

       ihh huh- huh- hu :h

                 •ih=

=•h h C̲o̲me o u t a g a̲i̲ :n

  •hehh   huh   hu̲ h hu

                 ple̲ a̲:se.

             hhe̲:h̲ heh

he h-eh

hhe̲:h̲ heh he h-eh

       When you comin' ou̲(h)t

aga in um r̲unnin a lih sh o̲:rt.ih h he̲h h e h

  mm-hm-hm-h u̲ h -h̲ u̲ h̲

                ih hn̲ ya ha

=•hhh I fill like hev'n a good ti:me. (I yiss)

             W'l'ee̲

W'l'ee̲ estuh

   uh ha̲ h   huh   hu

      u̲nh hu̲h hu nh

Ya̲nkee ehh-he̲h ha̲h ↑hah hah ∘huh-huh∘

           eh hi̲h hi̲h hi̲h hih

aa̲hh! huh

e hh!

  heh hehheh heh huh.

  Mhh! hmm hmm h eh!

   eh h̲i̲h!

uh h̲i̲h •hhh

    •∘e::::::::h:o::h.∘ ↑GI̲R:L.

=h hnh hnh? hua̲h ha h •∘ehhh∘

 ∘↑hih ↑hih hih.∘ Didn' I te(ll) y̲o̲u̲

all ah t↑o̲'d you . . .

  ∘ehh-huh-hih∘

∘ (h-m hm hm) ∘

hu -h heh he-h heh

 ∘heh heh h-eh∘

   eh huh huh huh heh heh hah hah

ehh↑ (h)O̲h(h)o he e Y(h) a(h) ah h̲a̲ h̲a̲

   huh huh

     ihh h̲i̲h heh heh

= h̲a̲ ↑ha

= heh •ehh

 ∘↑hn ↑hn∘ •h̲i̲h̲h̲ Ih wuz h ih huh

 •h e h h •i̲ h h h

 ihh: i h h : : h̲i̲h

(.)

ihhh: huh-h̲u̲

uh ↑h̲a̲ h̲a̲ ha- a̲h̲↑ ha ↓ha •ihhhh

W::ell ↑heh

 e̲h! h̲e̲h! heh he̲h hue̲h ha̲h hua̲h hua̲h.

uh -h! hheh heh heh heh -heh •hh

 eh teh (.)heh-h↑ih heh-h↑ih

                    (dz) Y<u>e</u>::::.   u:::::'ow you
ihh h   nh h↑ih   uh!
        nhh!
                    •◦uih::::::uk •ehh◦
◦(ih)A<u>w</u>::hh◦
                    hhh<u>h</u>eh- •<u>hheh</u>h
<u>r</u>o(ho)ck ↑heh   huh
↑ee↓YE: :↑E S ?   hh h<u>u</u>h heh heh=
                                •ehhh

eh Not th<u>e</u> f<u>loo</u>:h one
<u>e</u>hh::   <u>h</u>   <u>e</u>uh <u>he</u>   h-<u>heh</u>-<u>he</u>   h
        ehhh   h<u>e</u>:h   he:h •kkhh •hn
a(hh)r   (hh)ight th(h   h)en   •a h   •a h =
        •◦u   :   :   :◦   (<u>a</u>out thehr) it's
    •ah   •kh •<u>hh</u>e:hh
young <u>swin</u>gihs yih   nehhh heh   <u>heh</u>   •khu: =
                    O o <u>:</u> h   no: <u>O</u>h n-
eOh<u>:</u>?hhh heh heh •eh h: •h h h i : h
=hn   •hhh
   <u>B</u>hh   h<u>ah</u>   ↑huh   huh   •◦hh◦=
<u>O</u>hh <u>HA HA HA H A HA HA HA</u>   •↑Hooo=
=↑Hoh ↓n:<u>O.</u>   •↑h<u>uu</u>h
↑•hu   uh-huh
            (hh)ughn?   •hh yes ha ha   ha h uh
            ↑oh: ↑oh   ↑ohuh-hoo   ↑•uhhh-=
=   hoo
◦nh-h   uh◦
        hu hah hah   hah hah hah hah
                ↑hu::h- ↓huh

　　　　　　　　°↑huh hih-hih°=

=°↑uh-hunh!°

°hhh　::::::°

　　　↑O:h ↓no(h)o=

= (ehih uheh)

　　　↑hih-huh　hu↑AH!　huh-hah!

°↑hih　heh.°

ihh　huh　huh　•h::h

(t'sh)　　mh! hmhuh mhuh.

　　　　　　　　u-huh?=

huh huh　　huh　hh h ( )

　　　　　Yeahah h hah •hh=

　　　　　　　uh huh　huh huh

　　　　　　　　　　heh heh heh

　eh hah hah

You have pie:: tonight.　　　•hhh You have pie

ehhh hh n hn

ehh heh •hehh Ya:h •hnff•hh

(.)

•ehh Yeah I'm gonna go out an' get baked an' drink 'n nhhh

　　　　　　　　　　　• uhh •uhh •uhh •uh

　　　　　　　　　　　　heh hah　(• e u

h h)

Not when she di:ed, when she was born. Unih hnh ha •hh

　　　　　mi(h)ssiles ha　ha ha oozies

　　　　　uh- ha ha ha ha huh.

=•hhh No　I know yer no t, h h h h　•h h

　　　　　　　　heh, he-heh -heh-

heh-heh- heh- heh

```
         h h   heh   heh huh=
=•hhhhhh   I keep running te:sts onyuh I no
=ehh he-   heh-heh-heh-heh-heh    ◦hn◦=
                •h h h h h h
=UH::hhhhhhh No, nucle::ick I'vejust hh •hhhhhh been
=◦Hm um.◦ (hh)
                        >£ Hu- •hh h
He(g)h::: = ↑heh heh heh heh heh ↓hah hah hah
    hah hah hah
=Ha ha ↑HA::H £But nothing else ro    se  .£=
                                •hh
= Heh ha:h ha:h ha- ha- (eghk eghk eghk eghk)
= >Ha ha ha ha ha ha ha ha ha ha ha ha ha ha
•ih:gh::!< (.)::    gh-   o:::h,    b: a:d.=
                O::hh my £Go:::d. £
=But anywas, £s-huh huh. £> •hh So anyways
Eat'n? ehh heh   -heh
                (d)↑Ay hay(huh)
(d)↑Ay hay (huh dub) £eated.
•↑ehh hh
        No ↑I- I- I- already eated. hh-hh-heh
                    ◦hh-hh-hh◦
                    nh ha ↑ha ha ha.=
=•ehh=
•↑hu:hh. ↑huh-huh huh-huh. hih-uh-huh-uh◦
↑Huh-huh-huh-huh huh •hh
            eh ↑hih hih hn ↑hn •hhh=
•ehhh
◦↑nh nh nh hnh hnh◦
```

(0.8)

•hhh-hhh

(.)

↑eh heh Leave me a↑lo:::ne!

•ehh

(0.7)

ehh

(0.2)

°heh° hUhm gonna went home, said.=

=eh heh huh ↑hu

(0.5)

•kh-•hhh

(0.2)

hNo(h)o. ↑LA:UGH! ↑Cu:z. It's funny. . . .

Yeh- uhh hahh hahh   hu-•uhhh

  Hu huh u ha ha   ha ha ha ha

               Hhh h hhh   huh   huh   huh   huh

                  HAH HAH HAH HAH AHA=

  HAH HAH HAH HAH HAH HAH (.) •hh   huh huh

= huh huh • u h h h h   W↑e:ll.

       Ha ha ha ha ha ha ha ha ha •hh   •hh

=ehhh huh °hh°=

pt •hhh

((noise))

hih hih

ABATTLEHORSEANUDEWOMANANDANANECDOTE.

Remember that a picture, before being a battle horse, a nude woman, an anecdote or a whatnot, is essentially a flat surface covered with colours assembled in a certain order.
    —Maurice Denis

A.

you know like
when it's like
formulaic but like
you like like
the formula?

●

was like.
nature is.

ceramic panther.
bareback subject.

      (a) machines
      (b) other things

wars, journeys, shit like that...
food, danger, a mate, or whatever...

shark chum. a
soldier

sips of hot chocolate
after the tango battle.

after the ostrich joust.
simper the dreadlock pile.

boxes and boxes of. brains. put to
deed. a whole wall of what's wicked.

hubby martyr panel.
conference keyhole

address.
            oppressive stuff.

SKOOL
FAMLY
WERK

(
the acquisition
              of language a

        whole world ·
of what's wicked

●

socio. collab.
[*joke*] - laff

because the crowd
laffs not because

the joke's funny. is.
th'acq.-o-lang

.)

        sob
        track

lyric
voice

swallow
chalk

[*my*] eating
disorder   (*find it*

and i will buy you a pint of tripes

●

garburator frozen peas snac-pac microwave barfridge cable tv xbox
ceiling fan

nature is
nature is sculpture

nature is freezers dumped in the woods, munchies
noise music cupcakerias yoga tattoos small dogs nature is, recipe

apply a mixture of hamburger and butter
hamburger and butter applied to the face
mixed with cotton and tape
and tape a layer of flesh onto a head
then attempt to put the wig on
put the wig on top of that to cover the head
cover the head i
eventually became more interested in
interested in chocolate and mayonnaise and ketchup
ketchup chocolate being related to
excrement as is mustard is especially all natural mustard

●

nature is
watch as

    a plague of rabbits
    inveigle

    past my filters

the brutality of history

continues today... i married

a terrible photographer

made love to a bad poet

dated a lousy sculptor

courted an incompetent engineer

kissed a clumsy dancer

sucked-off a tone-deaf singer

a very talented

conceptual artist then
cleared away
the supper dishes

                Heidi
                I'm home

●

(8:15 is at 7:45)

(

    wormhole
    with a
    loophole

)

(

    oh

      so
you admit to throwing eggs

          (

            so
         many little eggies

         why just beggin'
         to be scrambled or fried
             [but weepy]

)

    (
      small circle of chairs
           inclu

    wide circle of chairs
        exclu

(i wanted
              to write
              a book
              i could
              read
              for
              the first
              time after
              having
                      written it   )

(9:55 ended at 7:45)

●

(**sauna truck**)
              [

                    my eyes
                    are wells of pain

(

              you just take the other person's
                    love and compassion and stuff &

              in your heart
              into the hole
                      crammit

)))))]

●

ca n 'tc   ope m u   st d
o p e   can't c ope m u
st   do do p   e   ca
n 't   c opemus   t d op
e   ca 't copemu s
tdodop e   ca n't c
opem us t do pe   c
an't   c opem u st d odo
p e   c an't c ope m ust
d o p e   can't c o p
em us t d o do pe   c
an 'tc   ope m ust   d   o
p e   ca n 'tc o
pe mus t   d od o pe
c an 'tc opem u·s t dod o
pe   ca n 't c op
em ust d o pe   ca
n 'tc opemu s   t d od op
e   c a n 'tc op e m
u   st do   p e   c a
n 'tc   o pe mu st   do d o p
e   c an 'tc ope
mus t d o pe m us t   d o
peca n 'tc   o   pe

95

someone?!? s/he
who do not care
what others think
will not bother say
ing s/he do not
care what others

think
really

careful
be

        there're
        theory mongrels there-
                over

    [*k*]

i don't understand how
you don't understand
what the sender
reckoned the receiver
would reckon the sender
would reckon

●

    communicable
    remarkable
        totally famous

ekphrastic
arrogant
huge
adequate
implausible
banal
well-regarded

obsolete as
      nature is

THEQRY.

•

SAME
diff
.

when
EVER
.

(

OBLIGATORY all caps

obligatory line

     break

     as
     such

     is a
     such thing

     as
       like
     a

     kick
     stand

     in
     sand
        :

     use
     less

)

     [*thigh slap*]

WE
DON'T
NEED

ART
.

WE DON'T NEED ART

ANYMORE

Q.

[Innerview]

Q: *[umn]* snuggle the
smuggle the
market into our
pockets moan in
in three *[e]*
expressive
registers
people
cry before all poems
start go went down to
sit down by
dogparke stream &
weep beseeched fleece
poetry needs
late lyric glut compass
fuller thoughts behind i
have no idea ownership
might be a loaded word
but why
more what's least
important to you in your
what gives
what do you
unjoy about writing
why
breathe
how many snows have you
survived
springs manurèd do
you read aloud

poems to your wife as
how easy does it
practice your product
b-movie b-poetry be
spoken
what it
do you
how who
are you a
poet round about yore
own beaten town?

A: o my voice says wherefrom
who i am i say
how i wannit to sound
a that was
very powerful reading
emote
[*r*] control
sense
wicked power reading but a
faint more willowy nest time
i [*feathery*] am all ways nervous i
dauntive mind to say
always always [*skirr*]
nervous i.

Q: is it for them to feel delight
forevermore somatic yew
dance dance on [*fur*] impact
notepad in the woods
spirit paperclip whole cloth
crazy at desk or oak walk?

A: i write about nature coz
i'm outside all the time it
art it just affirm

what is was living [*snuff*]
in the world as simply
nature was not an idea was
rocks & trees [*anideatrix*]
not to be written about
written about & discussed by they
who talk like musicians who think
they talk like philosophers in Simple
Times back then i will have been
one of Carl Sagan's future ex wives.

Q: poetry a formal spittoon loon lag
[*oon*] burdens success empíre
of cultural sadness first line
to pass [*blip*] thought someone
else share ore dignitaps
worry label torture intersoul?

A: people i yes my poem o
New York was killing me may
be i should get out Baltimore
Baltimore in it whence
loiterers daren't
go my poem is it
from a trip to Tofino
Tofino where blue is heavy
Tofino where wind blew so
such movement
through city reproduces city city
capital Scotland or someplace
very much hidden like the lithe
Sultanate of Sennar passed
has guided my pen evade
psychiatry till the people
who have been through
therapy identify
a slow stopwalk

as just how i roll that's so
[*mash*] more sense than i
plan to make
horizont
ology [*huf*]
as makes going passed
the horizon imaginable so
plannable
a new
line
is
a
new
occasion
first
pen
mark
[*bloody*]
on my
new shirt
not
anchored in [*scribble*]
narrative self-expression.

Q: could you go through
genesis a favourite
poem tastes clock
evolved amphibian flyover
windowpane novelists bang
whilst hurt poets watch?

A: i hesitate to [*con*] say
states of umsciousness a
thought
or none
pours pours
down

the page i'm
happy only happy
when it
pours
feel
time
of poem it
as time
it
happens the
information awl the
smoky old info [*ensnufflés*]
surrounds us just curious
[*cuss*] by the name of it.

Q: how've you coped with
all the sitting so much
sitting chair globule patch
hail of synonyms &
so petite [*insinuatory*
combustion] how did
you avoid being crushed?

A: i wrote a lot about the suburbs
very lonely i was i would
buy a little cabin in the woods
again [*n/n*] again
in cabin the woods all what
i got was frustrated
one eyed
on future
one eyed
on lyric
cross i all i got all [*x*]
very very destiny
just one a those things that
comes outta you.me

this is
me this is me
me as a writer & my
husband sleeps there too.

Q: a poet's goal to
make folk look [*dffrn't*]
a way in touch
orb glow delight is it enuff
tickletobey to build a tub
padd*lech*itecture dream reader sir
[*skfft*] o what's urgent now?

A: ohmg imho wanna make [*dunno*]
beautiful poems forthcoming book
Hieroglyphics Hindenburg erstwhile
book the Burger Clap i'm in
spired & amn't to my take
on it is i
don't think about it don't
think about
it don't think about
don't think poetry is
something i like it
something i like to
to like-read it we like
know what we like know
you know you know
part of my job [*descript*]
as looming moderator
lugubrious as we
is to feel a [*liddle*] more whispery feel
as probably griddlecake
middle very pro
bably i will batter &
hush a lot a people out o water
hush-off soft so bcuz

spoken in my own truth stand you
go on faith believe
hope think feel apprise why
we're fun
damental here embroider
a lotto ticket listen [*tt t t t*] the
pulse o the world arm beat
myself with detáils
detáils (anthropoid skulls, refrigerators...)
detáils detáils nicked [*kiosk*]
from the unadulterated rubber
undulatory natural world i admit
it yes o i admit it to be so.

THEQRY

Curtain.
A luxurious room, dominated by a long, heavy dining table surrounded with
ornate, uncomfortable-looking chairs.
  Downstage right is a standalone chess table with two chairs. Large,
misshapen chess pieces made of some ambiguous material that might be
marble, cheese or foam.
  Downstage left is an oversized rocking chair. Beside it is a sinister,
overflowing knitting basket, including a giant ball of yarn stuck with many
needles and stuck with an obviously fake, toy cavalry sword.
  The room is bursting with a dissonant collection of furniture and luxury
knick-knacks from many places and centuries. It should suggest a moneyed
colonial tastelessness that could be from any century, every century, or
no century at all. Items might include: replicas and representations of
pineapples, African masks, native North American artefacts, imitation
Louis XIV furniture covered in clear plastic, elaborate modernist ceramics,
abstract blown glass, imitation Ming Dynasty vases, endangered species
rugs, ostentatious stone urns, taxidermy, white marble statues. Decor must
conspicuously include costly, garish Christian paraphernalia; gold crucifixes,
silver churches, oil paintings of angels. Etc.
  Around, near, under, behind the furniture throughout the room, across
the stage, are SERVANTS clustered into groups. Throughout the play, the
many SERVANTS move variously like a pack of animals or a natural force,
sometimes with awesome unity, sometimes sharply divided. Some groom each
other. Some are sleeping. Some are being sexual. Some are lying in heaps.
When lone SERVANTS break away, they quickly re-merge. Many but not
all of the SERVANTS are reactive to what the dominant characters say and
do.
  Except for ISADORA, the dominant characters treat the SERVANTS
as invisible. Commands are addressed to the air, not directly to the
SERVANTS. Commands regarding treatment of ISADORA, should be seen
to create divisions among, and struggles between, the SERVANTS.
  The SERVANTS may be dressed in some kind of degrading uniform, like
fast food employees, or something uniformly drab. Or they may be dressed

in multiple, clashing styles of servitude that add to the visual and historical clutter.

MUSIC plays as the curtain opens. MUSIC will play throughout. Obligatory rests and obligatory changes in intensity are marked. The ensemble, like the decor, should be made up of instruments from disparate contexts. The MUSIC should be ambient, except where obligatory melody or percussion is marked. Suggestions for the ensemble: mixed percussion, ondes martenot, prepared harmonium, digeridoo, bass recorders, bass flutes, wine glasses, clarinet, double bass, harmonica, pan flute, kalimba, jaw harp, biwa, glockenspiel, celesta, nose flute, electric cello, slide guitar, synthesizers, glitch loops. Etc.

Enter a group of SERVANTS, chattering to each other with restrained excitement. They carry a stretcher bearing a heavy, minimum 4-foot tall, radiantly white BUST of Ludwig van Beethoven.

SERVANTS' *chatter. Improvise on*
Poet. Sculpture. Music. Magic power. Hearts. Revolt. Resistance. Sexual excitement. Trap. Contagion. Disease. Isadora.

SERVANTS erect the BUST on the table, upstage, face towards the audience. Some cluster to put extra structural support under the table, as if to help bear its weight. Some kiss the BUST's lips. One takes two small potted cacti from the stretcher and places them before the BUST, then spits drily into the pots as if to water the cacti. As they are doing this, another group of SERVANTS sets out five formal place settings on the table.

Enter DONNY and ISADORA. SERVANTS disperse, some nervously glance back and forth between ISADORA and the BUST.

DONNY enters with his back to the BUST and table. He is wearing impeccable formal dress with accessories: cufflinks, watch-chain, spats, diamond tie-clip. He is dragging along a resistant ISADORA.

Although ISADORA is addressed as feminine, her gender is visually ambiguous. She wears something dark and plain – perhaps a Nehru jacket, or gender-neutral, crisp pyjamas – through which her body type isn't readily legible. In her left hand she clutches a large leatherbound book. With her free hand she tries to resist DONNY by grabbing hold of furniture, in the process knocking over precious knick-knacks. SERVANTS scramble to clean up the mess.

DONNY

Come, Isadora. You must. Officer is coming for dinner again. Mother
wants to talk about your writing, again.

ISADORA

N-nnno. No! Please? Don't you love me?

DONNY

I do. But what about me? *[Agitated, nervous.]* You know I need to ask
Officer an important favour. He's a Great Editor, but a severe man. Help
me be brave.

*DONNY succeeds in compelling ISADORA to sit at the table with her book
before her. Still not noticing the BUST, DONNY takes a vanity mirror from
his inner pocket. He uses it to check his outfit and practice looking bold,
confident. He lightly powders his face.*

DONNY

Don't say anything creepy, Isadora. Listen to Officer's criticism – he
knows. *[Losing patience.]* Ack! You demon. Why did you get all the
talent? You just waste your gifts. Show more respect. You have to give
up this maniacal scribbling and those weird books. Be more feminine.
What if Officer wants to marry you to one of his 9 sons?

DONNY notices, in the reflection behind him, the BUST on the table.

DONNY, *turning*

Wh-what?

*Transfixed, he approaches the BUST. Unseen to DONNY, ISADORA
is looking at the BUST; smiles. She starts humming to herself. MUSIC
accompanies her. Melody.*

DONNY

Is it? Who is it? Mahler? No. Mozart? But that fiery hair. W-Why is this
here? Do you know anything about this? Hm, nice cacti. Did father
have this shipped? *[Touches the BUST.]* It's so – so cold.

ISADORA, *to herself, Sprechstimme*
A cold, black jelly hole. Fresh from kin.

DONNY doesn't hear ISADORA's answer. As he gets lost in contemplation of the BUST, SERVANTS, including some of those involved in carrying the BUST, gather under the table. ISADORA is willingly drawn down to join SERVANTS, where they cuddle, tickle, giggle, flirt and caress.

DONNY
It must be a gift for me. From whom? B-But I'm a poet. And it's far too small for my room. Did they deliver the wrong size? Bach? Or Wagner? D-Does it – does it matter?

DONNY runs his hand slowly over the face of the BUST, measuring its features. He touches his own face and head, comparing the BUST's features with his own.

DONNY
Could it? Will it? Will I be? Is there any f-future for poetry? A future not pain and death? C-can you have your own bust if you're not a German composer?

MUSIC stops abruptly. SERVANTS enter from offstage, carrying the first course of a meal of several courses, which will succeed in a desultory way. Foods are curious luxuries and/or aphrodisiacs: asparagus soup, artichoke, oysters, smoked eel, caviar, foie gras, quails' eggs. Fruit bowls of peaches, grapes, pomegranate, cherries. A single, uncut pineapple. Ample red wine.
    Enter MOTHER and OFFICER as the table is set. DONNY awakes from his reverie. His nervousness returns.
    OFFICER wears an antique military uniform of uncertain origin, with many medals and stumps of ribbons. Poorly tailored, it does not seem he's ever removed the uniform, either to shower, fuck, sleep or eat. In his 60s at the youngest, he is bone-skinny. An empty sword scabbard hangs from his belt. On his head he wears a ratty perruque. Throughout the play, he tries to conceal a jealous, agitated interest in the looming BUST.
    Voluptuous MOTHER wears a long, perhaps strapless evening dress, a diamond choker and other jewellery.

SERVANTS hoist reluctant ISADORA back into her chair. She is visibly sour.

OFFICER is quick to begin eating and drinking. Trite dinner MUSIC. Melody. Throughout dinner, SERVANTS fill the GHOST place-setting and replace each course as if it's being eaten, while sneaking bites for themselves.

Seating is in this order, from upstage: BUST; DONNY; GHOST; MOTHER; OFFICER; ISADORA.

ISADORA eats little. She feeds unchewed portions to SERVANTS under the table, like dogs. As the scene progresses, she becomes increasingly absorbed in her book.

DONNY also has trouble eating, but tries hard. He drinks more wine than it seems he would like, as if imitating OFFICER.

MOTHER eats precisely half of what she's served, and drinks nothing. She speaks about DONNY as if he's not in the room, paying attention only to ISADORA and OFFICER. MOTHER sometimes addresses the BUST when she speaks to OFFICER, conflating them.

OFFICER, *eating*
Ah, you spoil me, Mother.

MOTHER, *cleverly*
While my good Husband is away all the spoils of this house are yours, Officer. *[Indicating the GHOST place-setting.]* By God's grace, he is ever with us in spirit. What's this? *[She approaches the BUST]*. Mendelssohn? Schütz? Sent by your father? Who put this here? Isadora? My, but it's large. Handsome. Ooh, I like these cactuses or cacti. Is this a gift from you, Officer? Sit, young Donny.

OFFICER
Gift? *[Derisively.]* I'm not known for my gifts.

ISADORA, *to herself*
Mr. Numinous Sponger.

MOTHER, *sitting*
I asked you here again tonight to discuss the writings of my troubled child.

OFFICER

Indeed. Eel roe, so fresh! When do we dessert? Black Forest cake with cognac, as I ordered?

MOTHER

Her maids inform me she doesn't sleep or pray at night. In her room, she sits up late to write. Some nights I hear her laughing blasphemously to herself. In the day she mocks her brother – who I agree is pathetic, but it is not for her to judge.

DONNY, *to himself*

Pathetic?

MOTHER

When she comes out of her room, I see traces of tears on her face. Her face is flushed. With joy, fear, sorrow, I don't know. What if these tears are pity for her useless sibling? What if they are from nostalgia? Or orgasm?! I'm afraid of what she writes.

DONNY, *to himself*

Useless?

ISADORA, *to herself, resolved*

A little book of poems won't burn.

ISADORA tries to leave the table.

MOTHER

Isadora! *[To SERVANTS.]* Seat her.

SERVANTS coax ISADORA back into her seat.

MOTHER

Her poetry – or what she calls poetry – is indescribable. Donny, we both know, struggles with his hexameter but, we also know, will never make anything of it. Beneath notice.

DONNY, *to himself*

Beneath notice?

MOTHER

Like my critically acclaimed Husband, you, Officer, are prolific because
you sign your name to whatever well-turned poems are submitted to
your journal. You never write lazily, or strangely. My own miniature
poems, well, ha ha ha! *[Dissolves into titters and giggles.]* Hee heeee hee,
hee hhee heee hhhe heeeeee! *[Composing herself.]* But Isadora. She writes
lunacy. I can't ignore it. Immoral! Devilish. She writes like she's self-
taught, a creature.

DONNY, *to himself*

Pathetic. Useless. Beneath notice.

MOTHER

Like someone who needs neither teacher, nor workshop, nor editor, nor
confessor, no merciful God, nor discipline. Nor good husband. Not
even her own heart!

DONNY, *upset, talking to the BUST*
which he appears to hear speaking to him

There are no busts of women composers, anywhere. No woman can sing
or write.

MOTHER

Oh, she writes in a style I can neither place nor suppress. Help me. My
authority is ineffectual without yours.

ISADORA, *to herself, absorbed in her book*

Birthday party of a dying man.

OFFICER

Does she deny the laws of art?

MOTHER

She says things that burn my ears. Restless. She execrates.

DONNY, *to the BUST*
Write only what you know. Live like a lamprey, write like a lamb.

OFFICER
Is she heretical? Is she chaste? A virgin? Does she hate correctly, to amuse?

DONNY, *to the BUST*
Be meaty and muscular in prose, lean and sinewy in verse.

MOTHER
She hates only you. She sometimes says, without prompting, that society should be just, loving. She says old men are, er... Knee. Crow. File?

OFFICER
Necrophile?! Love of Solomon! Hmph.

MOTHER
Love? Solomon? Is gneee-krough-fayl like free love? O, to you, I – I am open.

DONNY, *to the BUST*
The wheat of verse must be separated from the chaff of doggerel. Or false coins will flood the realm. Who will build our poetry Ark of such timber?

ISADORA, *to herself*
Answers to answers; questions to questions; dust to dust.

ISADORA rises to leave. SERVANTS apologetically force her back into her seat.
OFFICER, *to ISADORA; sneers*
I'll have you know: the seed of old men pumps through the heart and veins of this economy.

MOTHER

She damns the Good Book for, er, miss-old-guy-knead? She says women are equal to men. Good taste is something about, er, hedge-money?

DONNY, *to the BUST*

Why play water polo without a net? A castle without a moat is moot. No great fortress lacks a canon. The young must learn by banging their masters.

ISADORA, *to herself*

Ghouls own the tools.

OFFICER, *rising*

Hush, hush. Hush. All! I must not hear these sounds, or I may have to take a more severe notice of this deviancy. Isadora has enough potential, and I can produce a surplus – with a little punishment. Sweet as this fresh pineapple. Fruit of exquisite instruments. If she doesn't suffer now, in body, her writings will suffer later. I shall calibrate an apt ordeal. *[Severely.]* May she acquiesce, or may she learn to knit. The topic is closed. *[Sits. Resumes eating.]*

MOTHER, *relieved, horny*

Oh, Officer.

DONNY, *to the BUST*

A poem's style must be commensurate with the gravity of its moral.

ISADORA, *to herself, exasperated*

More like zombies, thus far. This place is a bone-orchard. *[With finality.]* I'm out. *[She rises.]* Out. Now.

ISADORA makes a determined effort to leave.

MOTHER

Seat her and silence her!

SERVANTS force ISADORA back into her seat with difficulty. SERVANTS now tie ISADORA to her seat with yarn from the knitting basket. The yarn binding her is strung in unbroken lines from the knitting basket all the way across the stage, like clotheslines. With the same yarn they also gag ISADORA. One SERVANT adroitly confiscates her book. Some of the SERVANTS intervene physically, attempting to prevent this treatment of ISADORA, but they ultimately concede under the imperial gaze of MOTHER and OFFICER.

OFFICER

And now when your son wakes from his nap, please inform him I am ready to continue the game of chess we started three months ago. I have pushed my pawn to the last square but one. The next step gives me a queen.

SERVANTS shake DONNY out of his imaginary conversation with the BUST, and lead him, dazed, tipsy, to his seat at the chess table. Coming to, DONNY makes an effort to look destined for success, checking himself again in his vanity mirror. SERVANTS clear off the dining table, except for the BUST, cacti, pineapple, and the GHOST setting, the latter of which they now lay with fruit.

MOTHER, *referring to the chess game*

Have you been playing that long? Donny, the next step gives Officer a queen. Do not fail us. *[Makes her way to the rocking chair, where she takes up her knitting. She rocks gently.]*

OFFICER, *taking his seat at the chess table. To DONNY*

Are you ready to have your bones pulverised? I shall destroy you. I have your queen by the skirts. Soon I'll have your king's codpiece in my hand.

DONNY, *noticing ISADORA; a little shocked*

Tied you down? And g-gagged? *[Torn.]* Ah, well, maybe it's – maybe it's better this way.

ISADORA, *gagged*
Bhh-chh-cdhh-b. *[Struggling to remove the gag.]*

MOTHER
Shush, Isadora. You must leave this prattle, or learn to knit. You must study high quality, devout books. You need a positive role model, like our dear Officer.

OFFICER, *to DONNY*
I have you now, maggot!

MOTHER, *continuing from before*
It's a calamity. She terrifies our guests. *[Hungry for OFFICER's attention.]* Wednesday night – in front of every member of my Christian haiku club – she urinated on the carpet, and howled her gibberish.

ISADORA, *gagged*
Fgl-blhb-dblg-chbdd.

OFFICER, *reluctantly paying attention to MOTHER, but focused mainly on the game:*
But does she not have potential? I shall tell – lately I was forced to hurry to a miserable hovel near your home to arrest a dying drug addict –

MOTHER
Christ our Saviour! I washed the feet of thirteen beggars, on my knees, the week before I married their father, my good Husband. I could never stand to see a beggar again after that.

OFFICER
Associations are sometimes very strong, indeed. Check! But pray, listen–

ISADORA, *gagged*
Jmn-hdcb-hmnnnphgh-ghmnj!

DONNY

Speaking of alliances and associations, Officer, I just wanted, most
respectfully, if you have time, and don't mind, just wanted to ask you a
small favour –

OFFICER, *ignoring DONNY*

I went to that hovel, hearing that your daughter was already there. She
was scheming to upstage me. I shan't be upstaged, not in compassion,
religion, justice, nor poetry – it was imperative I hasten to remove him –

DONNY

My question is, just in case, if you don't mind, just wondering if,
perchance, even if only by accident, you –

OFFICER

Your daughter had gone of altruistic concern, otherwise uncalled, and
uncalled for. Certain it was to diminish me. Certain. Yet what struck me
most were her words, which –

ISADORA, *gagged*

Qsbgmnf-wqncdh-fglwsq.

DONNY

Have you had any chance, please be honest, not to rush you, I'm just
curious, mostly, and I understand, as you well know, if, with your many
duties –

OFFICER

Words of deepest consolation – mixed with a queer jargon of some
provenance, I –

ISADORA, *gagged; louder*

Rrrrrrrrrrgh! Xzrqvshk-dmjtn! Pkbbfjprrr!

DONNY

Ok, well, just say it, I'll just go ahead, no risk no return, boldness pays
dividends, it's just that, Sir, I want to ask, directly, my Lord, have you,

perchance, read the six short poems – military epigrams, really – six tiny poems, it wouldn't take but a glance –

OFFICER

I heard power in that voice. Eloquence. Full-breasted anger. I had been certain no one in this family save your Husband could write for a flagon of yak's dung. Not for a snuffbox of desiccated worm-castings, I tell you. Certain. Of course –

DONNY

The poems I submitted, most humbly, for possible publication, not to be presumptuous, of course, in your esteemed journal – internationally esteemed – Excellencia –

OFFICER

Normally I detest red, atheistic, pagan blather. But her first words were –

ISADORA, *gagged*

Jmnnmmmm!

OFFICER, *jumping to his feet, yelling at the chess board*

Check mate!

MOTHER

That's amazing. I didn't know Isadora liked chess or beggars so much that she would cry "check mate" when entering a poor person's home.

OFFICER

It was I said it, Mother. *[Triumphant. Rises and dances.]* Only I! Always I! I, I, I!

MOTHER

Holy saints. I thought you were supposed to say "pax vobiscum" or say –

ISADORA, *removes her gag; piercing scream*

Aieeeeee! Aaiieeeeeaeeee!

MUSIC rises to a frenzy.

MOTHER

Oh God. Again?!

DONNY, *to himself; weary, sarcastic*

Round and round.

MOTHER

No. No. Bring Xanax and flowers – now! *[Approaches ISADORA.]* Dear, dear, be calm, lingonberry. Pudding pop most cherished. My arctic heather.

DONNY, *to himself*

Vinegar-and-baking-soda volcano.

ISADORA, *commanding*

Out. Now. Ouuuuuut. Out! *[Shaking her seat violently.]*

SERVANTS rush to ISADORA and tear away the yarn that has bound her to the chair.
   ISADORA rises. Other SERVANTS come in from offstage with trays of sedatives and giant clusters of many-coloured roses. They approach ISADORA nervously.

ISADORA

No! Extinguish roses. Flowers of greasy posterboard. Alone alone. *[She tears up big handfuls of the roses, scatters them across the stage, along with much of the Xanax.]* Fresh anamnesia chrysanthemum. Mandrake body spray. Tulip petals low valley cries of enraged fauna. Poinsettias encircle me spit on me spit thick fermented gob of centuries. Waves of screams a climbing black river of speech!

During the sequence that follows, SERVANTS try several more times to approach ISADORA with drugs and roses. Each time, she rips up great handfuls of the flowers and scatters them along with Xanax. SERVANTS follow ISADORA, trying, with limited success, to sweep up the terrible mess as she makes it.

OFFICER, *annoyed*

Ah, she raves. To distract you from lauding my swift triumph over your feebleminded, talentless son. *[Tearful.]* The girl draws attention from me again. Oh! Again. *[Sighs grievously.]* I'm so lonely.

DONNY, *depressed*

She gets all the attention.

ISADORA, *wandering the stage*

Where am I what planet is this what earth? Inaccident of story. Inaccident of expiated victims. I can't be saved from collective memory. On the trail of metamorphoses drowned de-eyed de-tongued de-limbed. Womanhood humanity mother servitude bleeds. A marsh blooms in the forehead of a wound. This can't be home.

MOTHER

You are at home, with your family dear. Your older brother, liddle widdle teenie weenie Donnypoopypants is here. Officer is here. Your confessor punisher protector while father Husband is away. I am your mother. Don't you recognise us?

ISADORA

Empty house of mud of burnt eyes mud of scorched genitalia. Ground organ meat. Capsized eyes of magnetic palaver sauces. Futile to sharpen my voice here twisted into a horn of fog without stoplights. He brings me here to die. It is the house that hates poetry.

DONNY, *rising*

What you write isn't poetry.

ISADORA, *wandering*

What is beauty but the lacerated sign of a smile on the broken door of a face? Muzzled in the seat of listening. Full of nailfiles. I hear a vast improvisation of tornadoes sunstrokes maledictions. I taught this village to know itself to unbridle secret demons throw burning cymbals into a toothless crater. I acclimatised a tree of sulphuric lava for the abject. Afraid of afraid of myself! Cities leap from vomit like lambs. My word smashes the cheekbone of tombs. Tongue of lantern ash. My word none could tame. Speech no chemical can gird.

DONNY

It's all gibberish. Freak's porridge. *[Covers his ears and head.]* The word as mush!

MOTHER, *discouraged, takes a huge dose of Xanax from the floor for herself, which she washes down with an astonishing amount of red wine. She then retreats to the rocking chair to knit.*

MOTHER

She keeps saying words. And more. Words. The hurt comes. In the form of words. Endless words. Black current. Truthiness. Oh my good Husband, abortion is a mortal sin, but couldn't we have stuffed her in a plastic bag?

ISADORA

Squirrel fetus stew. Packet of shivers. This feast a grimoire of signs famine despair. My dinner table a heap of bones I sit in desolation my throne of rotted flesh crowned with mouse droppings confetti strange wedding procession. Landscape poisons me with the aconitine of its alphabet. Stitches anchor in my winking flesh by force of the effort to free myself. More than my cut-in-half torso my hemp-snapped neck the enemy needs my consent.

MOTHER, *knitting and rocking faster*

Her throat was so soft when she was a baby. Moist infant's lips. So easy to stop. Forever.

OFFICER, *angry, approaching ISADORA*

Tace concludam os tuum.

ISADORA

I breathe Englishly. Greek a field of contraband tainted rum. Collapsed

Latin all too well. *[Pulls off OFFICER's perruque and some of his medals, throwing them to the floor.]* Tinder phoenix inflatable sociolect. Flamethrowers ignite the shrub of my waist.

DONNY, *to himself*
I got better grades in Latin than you did.

OFFICER, *furious*
My medals. My wig. My digestion. She ruins the game. *[To MOTHER.]* You are to blame. Cease encouraging her with attention. Retire her to rest, to sleep. Desist in feeding her. *[Threatening.]* And the saints watch round her bed.

MOTHER
Oh no. No. No, no. N-no. No-o-o-o-o-oh. *[Knitting and rocking faster.]*

OFFICER
If you resist my command, I myself shall retire her. *[Moves to grab ISADORA.]*

DONNY, *alarmed, intervening*
Don't hurt her! She's just an enthusiast.

OFFICER, *over DONNY, at ISADORA*
Shatter your shins! I shall! Shatter your shins!

DONNY struggles to keep OFFICER from reaching ISADORA. Some SERVANTS step in to help DONNY. They all tussle. Finally, OFFICER is overpowered and deterred.

ISADORA, *wandering again, during the scuffle*
Who calls me? I am unknown. Never arrived. The minutes parade around me like emaciated wolves a flock of whipstrokes. Indocile subject imperfect victim. No outside to this circle. No margin. The house breathes breathes breathes murder. Halitosis. Freon. Nosebleed seats! *[Here, ISADORA's nose may bleed.]* No tuft of sleep no tuft of silence no mouthful of pillow foam hides a socialist god. Interlaced meowing

123

sprays my gag with musk. And so vengeance stands up straight its ear to the day touchscreen dust hornet drivel.

Deterred, OFFICER draws the toy sword out of MOTHER's ball of wool and expends his fury by repeatedly stabbing the wool ball.

OFFICER, *stabbing the wool with the toy sword*
Hag-seed! Be wracked with cramps! Ferrum! Lamina! Debent!

The sword eventually breaks.

DONNY, *to OFFICER*
You. *[To ISADORA.]* You! *[To MOTHER.]* You? *[To the BUST.]* You. *[To the GHOST place-setting.]* Y-You... How can you and you and you and you and you do this to me? Why me? Me!

MOTHER, *sobbing*
It's going to be ok. Everything is going to be alright. It's getting better all the time, a little chunkier every second.

ISADORA
Womanhood. Humankind. Refuse the unacceptable. Learn in the school of the warrens. Maggots in an iron lung won't copulate. Only hands untangle vines of ideation without contracture. Knock the vitrine of the sun break the glass explode a farm of venomous ants into malevolent winds. And love. Love will project on our eyes slides of burning horse barns. Equus. More than a beginning birth of a rancid womb. Populate the stars with meticulously serrated goodbyes. End the world of numbers. Words of love one world our world round-shouldered world of little spoons. Equal sisters will hold hands in vacant torture chambers. Days with their mien of slick assassins will strip themselves of weed sap. Prayer of cactus milk in thickets of thorny sky!

MOTHER
Poor thing, poor thing, poor poor thing. My beloved baby. Beautiful daughter. An angel. Frail. She's an angelberry. God's muffin. We should

have fed her to the pigs.

ISADORA approaches MOTHER. Stands over her menacingly. MUSIC: percussion.

ISADORA, *hateful*

What? Are? You? Knitting? Motherrrrrrr!?

MOTHER

Nothing. Nothing. Nothing at all. I never learned to knit. I just click the needles together. The horror. *[Knitting faster again.]* For solace.

ISADORA, *wandering*

A red hour of sharks red hour of premonitive nostalgia. Not silent! I will speak to my uneclipsed kin my future kin. Here are my loves hatreds! Sew roots in the orb of my strength. Centuries of night conjured against us. Ghosts phantoms spectres. Olid souls. We am I are not afraid strong arms long immense hands palmed callous. Rivers encircle my throat, bayous dangle from my ears. Alone in my skin, furniturial grotto. Leave me leave me to cry to exhaustion exquisite drunken cries of revolt! Aaieeeeeeeee!

ISADORA faints. MUSIC stops. Sound of some frightened SERVANTS weeping.

OFFICER

Indeed. To the floor with you. *[Spits on ISADORA. Sheathes what remains of the sword, recovers his medals.]* Why waste my Latin and logic on thee, who art incapable of both? Why indulge my compassion sweet-tooth?

The same SERVANTS who carried in the BUST now carry ISADORA away from the others, and make a kind of human divan for her, cradling her head. Many other SERVANTS gather around her, protectively.

OFFICER, *shrill*

I know the truth. I possess the truth. I embody the truth. I am the truth.

[Replaces his perruque, raises the sword stump.] And who will deny it now?

MOTHER

Not me. Not me. Nor, I'm sure, this boy. Donny, hurry up and believe.

DONNY, *torn*

I'm believing as fast as I can. But my faith will choke. Give me time to swallow.

OFFICER, *pompous, pious, drunk*

It is enough. We must lead with gentleness those whose steps find stumbling-blocks in the paths of grace. Pray with me that her eyes may yet be opened to glory and felicity, to a state where the exhaustless copiousness of divine benignity places the happy inmates above all those mean, and mundane anxieties, those petty and local wants, which. Ah. Hem. Verily, I feel some of those wants myself at this very moment. I am hoarse with speaking; and the intense heat of this struggle hath exhausted my strength. *[Sniffing ostensibly].* I think the buttered partridge I detect will be a most seasonal refreshment.

MOTHER, *commanding*

Partridge!

SERVANTS bring in a dish of roast partridge, which they set on the chess table, knocking over many of the game pieces.

OFFICER, *sitting to eat*

See how much I am exhausted with this episode. The zeal of your house has eaten me up. So I must eat.

DONNY, *bitterly, imitating OFFICER*

You and the zeal of the house should soon be quit, then. *[Himself, trying to seem authoritative.]* I warn you: my father returns.

MOTHER

Ha ha hee hup! Eaddup! Yup! O man. Giddieyup.

DONNY, *to MOTHER*

You too?

MOTHER

No, I had an oyster-bone, a pearl, a vole's toe-knuckle lodged in my sternum. Hup.

DONNY

You sound just like her. Ack. I have to get out of this room, this house. Out. Clear my head.

OFFICER, *to MOTHER*

You must control that fury, that harpy of a daughter. You must flay her alive if need be – with the manatee whip.

DONNY, *sarcastic, imitating OFFICER*

Spare the boiling oil, spoil the child?

OFFICER, *speaking with mouth full*

Indeed, there is never enough butter. More butter! And horseradish! Horseradish! *[These commands go unheeded by SERVANTS.]* Ah I should kettle and crush you all, but I am merciful. I am all-loving. Blindly just. I am the law. Compassionate, commanding. Who is more beautiful than I? Ahh.

DONNY

Officer, before you leave – y-you are leaving – I still have to ask a favour.

OFFICER

Ah, you know the time to ask a favour. You know I never could refuse you at a moment like this, when my heart is warmed, and softened, and expanded. Ahh. And glad, were it in my power to comply with it, but you see here – here are only bones. *[Indicating his dish of partridge bones. Losing interest in DONNY.]* In truth, it overcomes me. These tears. Ah, victory. *[Weeps.]* I do not often weep but on occasions like these, and then I weep abundantly, and am compelled to recruit my lack of moisture thus. *[Drinks, weeps, drinks, weeps, etc.]*

DONNY, *frustrated*

I don't want partridge. I need to ask you an important question – about the poems I submitted to you over three years ago. Three years! Ack. It doesn't matter what I ask, or when. No one here ever listens to anything I say. No one.

OFFICER, *to himself, reasoning*

The night is hot, and requires wine to slake my thirst. And wine is a provocative, and requires food to take away its deleterious and damnable qualities. And food, especially butter partridge with horseradish, is a stimulative nutritive, requiring drink again to absorb or neutralize the exciting qualities. A circle of logic, you see. *[Drinks.]* Cake and cognac are forthcoming, yes?

DONNY, *defeated*

I can't even try anymore.

Exhausted, DONNY embraces the BUST, as if for strength and support. He leans his whole weight on it, collapsing. MUSIC stops abruptly. There is a loud cracking sound, from where DONNY is. Self-absorbed, MOTHER and OFFICER don't appear to notice.

DONNY

Oh. What? What the hell – the h-heck is this made of?

A chunk of the BUST has broken off, and some of whatever it's made of has soiled DONNY's suit. Still cradled by SERVANTS, ISADORA begins to sing to herself. MUSIC gradually rises to accompany her singing. Melody.

ISADORA, *singing*

Oh, sweet, fresh sweetlard.

DONNY *examining BUST*

It's. It's grease. Lard. Cold bacon fat? But. *[Tastes.]* Sweet. Fried. Candy crust. Sugarfat. Fucking hell. Flash-fried sugarlard!

Starting with the detached chunk, DONNY begins to eat the BUST.

DONNY, *with mouth full*

Ah, what is this – this music? The music you told me about, Isadora? Music. It's love. Music is love.

Through the sequence that follows, DONNY eats with increasing appetite, ripping apart the BUST's face and head, crunching through the solid crust. His suit, accessories, hair and face become caked with the sugarlard.

DONNY

Great! Great! Great? Oh, honey flypaper. Most social when it seems least social. Upper limit. Sublime. Melodious.

DONNY now reaches a pocket in the centre of the BUST's head that contains a dark fruit jam. This jam oozes out of the face-hole like a carmine yolk, over the potted cacti.

DONNY

What? What's, what's this? More? Surprise? B-black jelly hole? I'm. I'm in. I'm in!

ISADORA, *Sprechstimme*

What's that sound in your eye, Donny? *[Singing.]* A gift of my gifts to thee. Sisterly gift from meeeeee!

DONNY, *ecstatic, not hearing ISADORA*

I've reached the centre. O I love you. I love you, Isadora. I wish I were you. I wish I were gay. I never asked to be born. Now. Glue trap! At the centre of all. All!

ISADORA, *singing*

Beeeeeethooooooovennnnnnnnaborrrrrrrtionnnnnnn.

DONNY, *eating the jam, intoxicated*

I think it is made of. Blackberry. Mozart liked to go picking blueberries in the summertime. Must be. Blueberry. True, true, true. Rather dark strawberry. Brahmsian. No, it, it, it must be blueberry. Pachelbel had a taste for salmonberries. No. It cannot be, not here. In this village, so little village. Far from the city. There are no such berries here, on this whole Earth. *[Jolly fatherly voice.]* My boy, my son, do you really think it's loganberry? Ho ho ho. *[Malicious fatherly voice.]* You fucking moron. *[His own voice.]* What is the key of it, what key is it? What key? Secret? No, but I do think it's blackberry. Not blackcurrant. Açaï.

> ISADORA, *Sprechstimme*

Dingleberry!

> SERVANTS around ISADORA, *giggling*

Hee hee hee hee!

> DONNY, *very excited*

Black. Berry! Richard Strauss was an ass-pinching booger-eating dirty sot. Berg lanced a boil with lead scissors – dead. Webern shot by an illiterate American soldier. Control freak Schönberg cuckolded by a mediocre plumber. Schumann hanged by his fingers. Hrgh hah. If you answered yes to these questions, you just aborted Ludwig van Beethoven.

> ISADORA and DONNY, *in unison*

Congratulations!

SERVANTS *around* ISADORA, *with congratulatory hugs and kisses*
Ha ha hee hee hee hee hee heeho hee ha ha!

MUSIC: atonal music. Melody.

> DONNY, *snapping out of it*

T-That sound. No. W-who plays that strange instrument? But. What!? What is this guck all over me? What am I doing? Stuck. Ack! N-no! *[Ineffectually trying to clean himself off.]* Uh. No! *[Angrily pushes the BUST off the table. Its remains smash open on the floor. He sits down atop the mess.]* Destroyed. I am completely useless.

OFFICER, *noticing DONNY*
Hm, perhaps winds of potential do blow with him, if faintly.

MOTHER, *shaky, timid, very inebriated*
Officer, I know you are exhausted, but I must also ask you a favour.

OFFICER, *magnanimous*
Ask – 'tis granted.

MOTHER
I just wish to know one thing. Will all the people in the world who are not Christians be damned? Forever? And the untalented? Autodidacts? Slow learners?

OFFICER
Damned everlasting, without a doubt. The lot! Drink to it. *[Offers.]*

MOTHER
You know very well I never drink alcohol or take drugs, Lord have mercy.

OFFICER
I on your behalf, then. *[Drinks.]*

MOTHER
W-will they be in solitary confinement?

OFFICER
Lonesome as a ghost gnat's flatulence. As 12-tone cowboy lieder. Be reassured.

MOTHER
Merciful. Tonight I'll sleep. But – damned to all eternity, Officer? All?

OFFICER, *giddy*
All. All. All. All. All. All! Dungeon is forever. Hee Ho ho hoh. I know. I would have none other employment. Borrrnnn to this job. Ho ho ho ho ho hah.

MOTHER, *relieved*

Indeeeeeed! Haa ha ha hha ha ha hah ha.

DONNY

Oh? Hrrrphmgh. You. Ho ho ha. Do you have it harharhrrha too?
Contagious. Ha ha ha ha ha ha hah.

ISADORA, *cackling*

Hee hee hee hee hee hee hee hee.

SERVANTS

Ah ha ha ha ha hee hee hee hee hee hee hee hee hee.

ALL

Ha hee ho hee hee ha ho ha hee ho hee hee ha ho ha ha hee ho hee hee
ha ho ha ha!

*ALL laugh simultaneously, but each in a distinct humour, as if each laughs
for a different reason. For example, DONNY may laugh drily, bitterly;
OFFICER triumphantly; MOTHER could titter maniacally; ISADORA
and SERVANTS laugh with celebratory glee.*

*While ALL are still laughing, enter a lone SERVANT from offstage,
bearing a letter. Struggling to not laugh, the SERVANT goes to set the letter
at the GHOST place-setting, but finds fruit there. SERVANT puzzles, then
dumps the fruit over DONNY's head, perhaps intentionally, perhaps not.
SERVANT then lays the letter across the empty dish. Exit.*

MOTHER, *flustered, trying to regain control of herself*

My, my. Aha hha ha. *[Rises, wobbly, to retrieve the letter.]* Wha ha hahhr
what's this? It's a letter from your beloved father. Listen. Ha ha ha. Oo.
Sh-Silence. I said listen! Ha hah. Listen. *[Laughter is gradually quenched.]*
A letter from my good Husband, who has been away these long years,
dear God, only to provide for our modest needs. Hmm hmphrmph
hee hee. Ah. *[Reading.]* He says... Oh! His poetic assignment has been
extended another 8 months. And something about the, er, field of. Cult
Tour... All... Pro... Duck... Tion? Ducks? He, er – the handwriting is poor
– the paper is soggy – he... sends... his regards... from, from... Can't read

the name. He has enclosed... my oh... yes. A little poem! O, it's quite legible. Would you like to hear it?

Curtain.

INDEXICAL SIGNATURE

Before me

stretches, to my

left,

bordered on

each side, in

the distance, to

my right, on

the ground, there,

at the near

end,

down, come

close,

to us, in

the middle, quite

lately, stands,

here, on

another

side, closer

to me, right

in front of, but

lower, over

the whole scene,

while, in detail

nearby, behind

a screen, seen

from behind, and

to the right,

opposite, after

us, a foot

beyond them

starts,

at the far

end, north,

a distance,

inside, next,

at our

right and our left,

stretch, at first

glance,

the foreground

waste, next of

which, on

top of, to

the left, nearby

right, at the back, off

to one side,

below, set in

here, this

radiant place,

may be

filth, left,

right, further

on, one joins

us, look

up, turn, look

along

the void,

tourist,

until I

notice, already,

then shift,

as, here,

pleasure again,

calm

and

vigilant,

past the first, to one

side, just

opposite we

come, finally, at

last, next

to me, beside,

faces, hands,

feet, all

eyes now

turn, lower,

down the same

page, flat as,

beyond, set

down in a circle,

blinking, featureless,

a ground

moves,

dissolves

colourless, beneath

a, not outside, faded

edge, on the

other end, a

confluence

unravels, the

usual

flashes, in

a clearing,

there.

NOTES & ACKNOWLEDGEMENTS

If the loitersacke *be gone springing into a taverne, I'll fetch him reeling out.*
                                                            –J. Lyly, 1594

Loitersack started in 2006, with the desire to compile a commonplace book for my own and others' use. As it is now, my best guesstimate is that *Loitersack* is about 32.7 percent original thought, maybe 64.3 percent paraphrase, echo, transcription or collage, with at least 9.6 percent don't-really-know.

A *loitersacke* is "A loiterer, a lazy fellow [...] The adjunct *sack* seems to denote an inert or lumpish person" (R. Nares et al.). As a compound of loiter + sack, I also imagine a knobbly bag of enstrangements [*l'autre sac*] or burdens picked up while stealing time loitering around a university library, mainly among the stacks but also in the smoker's pit outside and at boozecans nearby. A spatial practice long criminalised as part of the criminalisation of poverty and non-whiteness, loitering suggests a simmering threat of ambush, sedition, or defiant anti-productivity. Unlike the window-shopping *dérive*, the thrift store *chiffonnier* or the multi-cappuccino *flâneur* – which now consumeristically "go with the [*capital*] flow" of the city – loitering can be thought of as producing motivated blockages in urban flows, and/or diversion of such flows into ambivalent alterities.

The main substantive editor of this book was [*gold*] Louis Cabri. Many other friends also contributed their readings of these texts in progress. I count over 40, which is more than I can name and still risk neglecting someone. I hope you can see my uptake of your input into the substance of these pieces as a demonstration of my appreciation, respect and gratitude. I have listened, and do listen. I can never thank you enough.

"The Young Hate Us": locally, a distillation of the issues (that have been) in play for me when making text-based visual art and concrete poetry. Generally, an outline of a [*neo*] social-materialist poetics.

"Whisper Sweet Notations": a poem of bad jokes and negations, to help open [*wormhole with a loophole*] spaces of ideological possibility.

Includes material from Charles Altieri, Clint Burnham, Jeff Derksen, Antonio Gramsci, Henri Lefebvre, Vladimir Mayakovsky, Ted Nugent and Harry Partch.

"Snowball in Hell Turns to Billiard Ball": outline of an ars poetica, pursuant to "The Young Hate Us." Thanks to Louis Cabri for the [*importn't*] "nonce word" versus "coinage" distinction. "IN/OUT" is an exchange with Gustave Morin. Morin's words are "IN". Thanks also to rob mclennan, Adam Seelig and Daniel Zomparelli; material produced for interviews with each of them is incorporated here and reworked.

"Biwrixle": a writing-through of Osip Mandelstam's "A Journey to Armenia" (1933), as translated by Clarence Brown in *The Noise of Time* (2002). *Biwrixle* is a Middle English word meaning: to change, transform.

"Laugh Particles": a direct re-transcription [•*hnff*•*hh*] of all the laughter transcribed in Phillip Glenn's book *Laughter in Interaction*.

"Abattlehorseanudewomanandananecdote.": draws together strands of several apparently contradictory or exclusive poetics discourses, attempting to make them eat, digest and excrete each other. The format is that of a poetry reading, followed by a Q&A

"THEQRY": is mainly an adaptation-perversion of Chapter XX (Vol.III) of Charles Maturin's *Melmoth the Wanderer* (1820). To this I've added material from my own translations and transpositions of Aimé Césaire's *And The Dogs Were Silent* (1956), along with cribs (of lines and motifs) from many [*many*] other plays.

"Indexical Signature": a writing-through of Raymond Roussel's *Impressions of Africa* (1910) (trans. Mark Polizzotti, 2011), Robert Byron's *The Road to Oxiana* (1937), and Bruce Chatwin's *The Songlines* (1986). Thanks to Janet Giltrow for giving me the poem's title: "Your poem – it's the indexical signature of travel writing!!!"

Versions of or parts of some of these texts were first published in: *Armed Cell, The Capilano Review, Event, The Last Vispo Anthology, Poetic Front, 17 seconds, Tripwire, W2010, West Coast Line*, and *Where Eagles Dare*. Thanks to the editors.